Deric Longden was born in Chesterfield in 1936 and married Diana Hill in 1957. They had two children, Sally and Nicholas. After various jobs he took over a small factory making lingerie, but he began writing and broadcasting in the 1970s and before long was writing regularly for programmes like *Does He Take Sugar?* and broadcasting on *Woman's Hour,* most of his work being closely based on his own experience. The demands made on him by Diana's illness, subsequently believed to be a form of ME, forced him to sell the factory, and since then he has devoted himself to writing, broadcasting, lecturing and after-dinner speaking. *Diana's Story,* published in 1989 some years after Diana's death, was a bestseller. His other books, *Lost For Words, The Cat Who Came In From the Cold, I'm A Stranger Here Myself* and *Enough to Make a Cat Laugh,* are also available in Corgi paperback. Deric Longden married the writer Aileen Armitage in 1990 and now lives in Huddersfield.

D0522611

Also by Deric Longden

DIANA'S STORY
THE CAT WHO CAME IN FROM THE COLD
I'M A STRANGER HERE MYSELF
ENOUGH TO MAKE A CAT LAUGH

and published by Corgi Books

LOST FOR WORDS

Deric Longden

CORGI BOOKS

LOST FOR WORDS
A CORGI BOOK: 0 552 13942 2

Originally published in Great Britain by Bantam Press,
a division of Transworld Publishers Ltd

PRINTING HISTORY
Bantam Press edition published 1991
Corgi edition published 1992
Corgi edition reissued 1993
Corgi edition reprinted 1993
Corgi edition reprinted 1995
Corgi edition reprinted 1996
Corgi edition reprinted 1997

This book is set in 10/11 Palatino by
Chippendale Type Ltd, Otley, West Yorkshire.

Corgi Books are published by Transworld Publishers Ltd.,
61-63 Uxbridge Road, London W5 5SA,
in Australia by Transworld Publishers (Australia) Pty. Ltd.,
15-25 Helles Avenue, Moorebank, NSW 2170,
and in New Zealand by Transworld Publishers (N.Z.) Ltd.,
3 William Pickering Drive, Albany, Auckland.

Printed and bound in Great Britain by
Mackays of Chatham PLC, Chatham, Kent

For Sally and Nick
for their love and understanding
For Aileen – for the rest of my life

Chapter 1

I would have recognized that backside anywhere. It loomed large above the surprisingly slim ankles, waited impatiently as the arms transferred parcels, one to the other, and then it swivelled and slammed into the glass doors before charging triumphantly backwards into Marks & Spencer, dragging my mother along in its wake.

From across the road I shouted but only caught the attention of a small, neat man whose hat had been knocked off in her backwash and by the time I entered the store she had disappeared into the crowd.

I studied my list. It was short and to the point. Tea, sugar, milk and coffee – a reflection of the grey that had entered my life since Diana had died and taken all the colour with her. In those days a shopping list had been a challenge.

'What's this?'

'Vine leaves.'

'Where will I get those?'

'Try that little shop in the market.'

The assistant had greeted me with a confident smile and slipped back behind her counter.

'Do you have any vine leaves?'

The smile shuffled itself into a frown as she turned to study the shelves.

'No – I don't think so. We've got Benson and Hedges, Silk Cut, Embassy . . . '

I kept a weather eye open for my mother as I tried to part a couple of wire baskets that seemed to be mating with one another. A violent tug wrenched four of the

7

damn things free and they hung there, copulating, from my wrist. I plonked them back on the heap in disgust and then an old lady said, 'Excuse me' and plucked the top one from the pile.

I tried again and this time found myself clutching a trio that appeared to be welded together for life. I could do without a wire basket, I only needed tea, sugar, milk and coffee.

Why don't Marks & Spencer sell sugar? This is one of the mysteries of life. They would sell mountains of the stuff – but then perhaps it would make the store look untidy and we couldn't have that.

I dreaded the confrontation with the sarcastic Beryl in the corner shop as I called for sugar on my way home.

'Been to Marks & Spencer again, have we?'

' . . . and a tin of beans.'

'We don't need charity.'

I tried to put Beryl out of my mind as I jumped on the escalator going up.

My mother was on the escalator coming down and for a split second we were eyeball to eyeball. I smiled and said, 'Hello, love.' She nodded politely, but looked straight through me and the distant smile on her face told me that she knew me, but she just couldn't place me.

She had travelled a couple of yards before it dawned on her that it was her son who had just spoken to her and she turned and waved her carrier bag in recognition.

As she did, a carton of black cherry yoghurt and a half a pound of best butter flew out of the top of the bag and beat her to the bottom of the escalator by about six seconds.

From my elevated position I watched as she took one step off the escalator, bent down to pick up the butter, and then began scraping the yoghurt back into the carton with the lid.

8

The backside presented an impenetrable barrier and behind her, about thirty fellow travellers were jammed like sardines, all of them running on the spot in an attempt to remain upright, and even more were piling up behind.

As soon as I reached the top of the escalator I joined the queue that was on its way down. The dam suddenly cracked open and I could see bodies squirting off the end as though they were being hurled into space – and then, three quarters of the way down I passed my mother going up.

This time she recognized me straight away. 'Be careful,' she shouted, 'it's ever so slippy at the bottom.' And, my God, it was.

There was yoghurt everywhere. A gaggle of women stood on one leg as they tried to scrape it off their shoes and their white faces told me that they had just passed through the valley of the shadow of death.

Yoghurt footprints trailed off in all directions and already an assistant with mop and bucket was trying to straighten out the mess.

'You can tell it's the football season,' he grumbled, 'they want locking up.'

'It's the parents I blame,' added another voice and I jumped on the escalator going up to see if I could find this seventy-two-year-old hooligan who had started it all. I thought, 'If I pass her going down – I'll strangle her.'

But no. She was sitting on another pile of wire baskets, completely oblivious to the fact that several people were trying to prise them out from underneath her.

'The lid wasn't on properly,' she told me and I suggested that perhaps they didn't design yoghurt cartons so that they could be hurled forty foot down escalators without exploding.

'And look,' she exclaimed, brandishing a silver lid with 'Sell by 14 March' written on it. 'It was out of date.'

'Today's the twelfth.'

'Shall I go and tell them?'

'No – I think you've made your point,' I said, and gently steered her away from what was now a rather flat pile of wire baskets.

'How about a coffee?' I asked once we were outside the store. She thought that was a lovely idea and I took her hand to guide her towards the little shop in the Shambles where they had checked table-cloths and wholemeal scones.

She had other ideas and frog-marched me across the road and in through the door of a café that served hot sweet tea through a hatch in the wall to customers who had to pay hard cash before the mug was placed within their reach.

'Usual, Babs?' asked a voice through the hole.

'Yes, please.'

'What about him?'

'Same again with three sugars and a bag of crisps.'

The place was alive with football supporters, punctuated by old men reading the *Sporting Life* and faded women who looked up enquiringly as I passed.

My mother beamed at everyone. This was the woman whose idea of heaven was to tour the teashops of Harrogate eating salmon and cucumber sandwiches with the crusts cut off.

'I like it here,' said my mother. 'People talk to you – they don't whisper.'

'Top of the morning to you, Babs,' shouted an old Irishman wearing a torn jacket and somebody else's trousers.

'Morning, Ben,' she shouted back and then added in my ear, 'He's Scottish today – he was an Australian last week. He likes a change.'

There wasn't an empty table in the place, but my mother sailed over to a corner where half a dozen football supporters held court. They glared at her as she approached and spread themselves on the bench seat.

'Nobody sitting here is there, love?' she asked a tattooed bovver boy with a football scarf tied around his wrist and Doc Marten boots the size of skips on his feet. Then, before he could answer, she had plonked herself down beside him and the backside cracked like a piston, ramming him and his two mates up hard against the plate-glass window. I perched myself gingerly on the end.

'You can only sit here if you're a Sheffield Wednesday supporter,' muttered the humanoid.

'My cat watches "Match of the Day",' declared my mother, 'but I prefer the wrestling myself.' I watched his eyes glaze over as she embarked on a monologue bespattered with references to Mick McManus and the various technicalities concerning the flying buttocks.

They loved her and I couldn't help thinking that if the police put my mother on a white horse and armed her with a loaded carton of black cherry yoghurt, she could bring crowd control down to a fine art, single handed.

'Ben over there,' she pointed to the old man who was staring into an empty mug, 'he used to play for Glasgow Rangers.'

In no time Ben was surrounded by newly found fans and no sooner had he demonstrated the finer points of trapping a crisp packet with his left foot than he was warming his fingers around a fresh mug of tea.

The café was now full to overflowing with Sheffield Wednesday supporters and I timed our exit just as my mother was about to join in the second chorus of 'You'll never walk again'.

I offered her a lift home and she accepted and we walked together towards the car.

'Did he really play for Glasgow Rangers?'

'I shouldn't think so – he came over from Poland during the war.'

This must have been the first time we had walked through town together since she took me shopping with her as a little boy.

I hated it then. It usually meant that I had to try on new clothes – grey school shorts that I would grow into eventually. It was a false economy, they always wore out before I grew into them and it spoilt the thrill of having that first pair of long trousers. I felt that I had always worn long trousers because the hem of my shorts always touched the top of my socks.

But even worse than shopping for shorts was bumping into Nellie Elliot and her piles. I would stand for hours while they nattered away fourteen to the dozen. You can see the same boredom mirrored on the faces of dogs caught in the same predicament, but at least a dog can sit down, wrap its back leg around its neck and lick its bottom.

I would stand there, my mother hanging on to my left hand, my arm pointing towards the heavens. I never used to have any blood in my left arm.

And Nellie Elliot and her piles seemed to hide around every corner waiting to pounce on us – wherever we went, there was Nellie Elliot and her piles. She had an obsession about them – she would describe them graphically. I remember the phrase, 'a bunch of grapes', being sprinkled liberally throughout any conversation.

But today it was a different story. The little lad had a car now and I squired my mother across the town, steering her through the hordes of football supporters, apologizing to those she had poked in the eye with her umbrella.

It was all so very pleasant and then my mother stopped, turned and walked over to a little old

12

lady who was wearing a Harris tweed suit and a crimplene face.

My mother smiled and introduced us. 'Deric,' she said. 'You won't remember Nellie Elliot, will you?'

Chapter 2

While Nellie Elliot was very real, my father was a shadowy figure in those early years – a man who came home every now and then and damped down all the fun in the house.

He hadn't wanted to go to war. Undertakers would be needed here, he had said, but after a lot of fuss he was persuaded to join the National Fire Service. He wrote to us twice a week and always referred to me as 'his little man', which was nice since he very rarely spoke to me when he was at home. He told my mother he loved her and missed her very much. We liked it when he was away.

'Take that off and listen – your father's written from the front.' I dumped my Mickey Mouse gas mask down beside my porridge, picked up a spoon and began to sort out the lumps.

In the early days this writing from the front business had confused me. Everybody writes from the front – it's not natural to write from the back. Then, as I took on the maturity of a five year old, I began to understand.

To the historian, the various fronts moved as the war progressed – there were several fronts. To my mother however the front remained constant. It was in Louth in Lincolnshire. Perhaps she was banking on Hitler massing his 45th Panzer Division just outside Horncastle, in which case my father would have been in the thick of it.

'He says that you are the man of the house now . . . '
He always said that.

'. . . and he says that he misses me very much.'
He always said that as well. '. . . and he hopes that
we are missing him.'

We looked at one another and said nothing and
that said everything. 'Anyway, that's about it really
– he's nearly finished you a carving and he's bringing
it home with him next time.'

Another bust of Shakespeare. My father believed in
working at something until you got it right. His early
attempts at the Bard had a look of the young Max Wall
about them, but he had persevered and now even I,
his sternest critic, had to admit that he had it just
about right. We had twenty-seven assorted carvings
of Shakespeare around the house – twenty-six of them
were in my room.

'Where do you think it would look best?'
'In Deric's room – he'd be hurt if not.'

I went along with it. Most nights I dreamt of
Shakespeare. Shakespeare scoring the winning goal
at Wembley – a hundred before lunch at Lord's.
Shakespeare wiping out a German machine-gun nest
single handed. And in the morning he would have me
surrounded. I had no idea who he was really, only that
he was in the Fire Service with my father at Louth.

I pushed back the rubber straps of my gas mask,
slipped it over my face and began to count the lumps
of porridge on the edge of my plate.

If I counted the walnut-sized lump as two, then I had
seven and my mother had six. I had won again. We
always did this – my mother said it was educational.

I took my cricket bat from the umbrella stand
and went off to play in the coffin on the front-
room rug. For several days now I had paddled my
canoe nearer and nearer to the German submarine
which was moored just off the Norwegian coast
by the coal bucket. The crew were too busy tor-
turing the captured fishermen to notice my stealthy

15

progress and my gas mask rendered their radar ineffective.

'I wish you wouldn't wear that gas mask all the time – you'll suffocate . . . '

She didn't understand.

' . . . and I want to work on your costume this morning – so don't go very far.'

The tide carried me silently over the hearthrug and into the mouth of the fjord. The cold was biting into my bones and I was glad I had eaten my porridge.

She had worked on the costume for several weeks now, building up the papier mâché inch by inch until I looked like a human ping-pong ball with two little legs sticking out of the bottom.

'What's he supposed to be again?' asked my Uncle Len.

'A Brussels sprout,' my mother told him. 'Keep still, Deric, this is a difficult bit.'

My Aunty Polly fed me a sweet through the eyehole. There were two eyeholes, but since they were about a foot apart, I could only see through one at a time.

Polly fed the sweet through the wrong eyehole and it fell to the floor. She tried again.

'In *A Midsummer Night's Dream*? I didn't know they had a Brussels sprout in *A Midsummer Night's Dream*.'

My mother dipped her paintbrush into the bright green Walpamur. 'He'll be symbolic – you know how they muck about with things these days. He probably heralds the coming of spring or something.'

I looked more like a small cabbage than a Brussels sprout, but I wasn't worried – I trusted her.

Around tea-time the next day Len parked his van outside the house. Usually I ran to meet him but today I had to concentrate on standing upright.

'He'll have to go in the back – he'll never fit in the front.'

As I waddled between them down the narrow passageway towards the front gate Len shouted instructions at me through the eyeholes and then picked me up as I fell over the miniature privet.

'They're too young to put on *A Midsummer Night's Dream*.'

'It's not his school, he's been loaned out to the Central.'

'Just him?'

'No – there's five of them.'

They bundled me into the back of the ancient van and Len jerked it into action. It took off like a cat, wiggling its bottom half a dozen times before making a break for it. We shot to the top of Heaton Street and then Len slammed on the brakes so that my mother could climb into the back to steady me. I was on my fifth circuit of the van's interior by this time – I knew it now like the back of my hand, especially the door handle and the sharp bit where the jack was stowed in a leather pouch.

I was spinning like a top as my mother opened the back door. She steadied me with her foot and then jammed me up against the spare wheel before banging on the wall of the cab and once again Len set off for the Central School.

My mother waved goodbye to him from the top of the steep playground and I winked at him through my eyehole before she manoeuvred me down towards the gymnasium door.

Inside it was all noise and excitement with people shouting and hammering and through my hole I could see a donkey with legs like mine and I began to feel at home.

Over by the stage, sitting prissily on a wooden bench, were my four class-mates dressed as fairies. Miss Woodward, my teacher, turned as they stared at me. She came over.

'What is it, Mrs Longden?'

17

'It's Deric,' my mother told her.

'I know it's Deric, but what's he supposed to be?'

'He's a Brussels sprout . . . ' The hesitation in my mother's voice half acknowledged that all was not well. ' . . . that's what you said.'

Miss Woodward's sigh was deep and unforgiving. 'I said a sprite, Mrs Longden, a sprite.'

We walked home. Len wasn't due back with the van until half past nine and we couldn't wait until then. I had wanted to stay and talk to the donkey but my mother said it was better if we left.

It was about a mile and a half on foot, we could slip through the twitchel, but it was hard going. The hedge on either side was overgrown and the stile presented problems for a five-year-old Brussels sprout; so my mother punched a hole through the papier mâché and I stuck my arm out and she hauled me over the top.

The rain caught us with still a mile to go. It fell in chunks and my mother was soaked to the skin in no time. It was a good job I was wearing my costume. The donkey had said we could leave it there with him, he'd give it to Len when he came for us.

'We can't,' my mother told him, 'he's only wearing his vest and pants underneath.'

I was as dry as a bone – the green Walpamur began to run down my legs and left a snail-trail behind us, but the papier mâché was a credit to my mother's craftsmanship and although it softened and I gradually turned into the shape of an onion, it held together until I waddled in through the front gate once more and fell over the miniature privet.

We sat in front of the coal fire and drank cocoa while my mother dried her hair. She had been quiet on the way home but now she pulled the dressing gown tight around her and said, 'I'm sorry about tonight . . . '

I couldn't see why she should be – I'd enjoyed it.

18

' . . . I can never understand a word she says – she's from Market Harborough.'

That explained it, then.

'Will you be all right at school tomorrow?'

I'd be fine. I warmed my hands around my mug and thought of Neville and John and Margaret Base and her sister Mary sitting on that bench dressed as fairies. I could pull their legs tomorrow – they'd looked a right bunch of idiots.

Chapter 3

'Do you remember the Brussels sprout?'

As I held open the passenger door she looked up at me blankly from where she lay across the two front seats of the Citroën.

'The one you made for me when I was little.'

I bent forward to help as she shimmied horizontally towards me, her skirt riding up around her waist, the gearstick gradually disappearing up her coat sleeve.

'I think I'm stuck.'

'Go back again.'

Her knickers blinked in the sunlight and then crept back under the check skirt as she reversed the process and lay once more with the steering-wheel an inch above her nose.

'Shall I try this one?' she asked, her eyes indicating the driver's door over her head.

'No, come on.'

I reached out and took hold of her hands. She always had this trouble – she couldn't swing her legs round without falling over backwards and if I pulled on her ankles, her clothes turtled up around her neck. A shovel would have been handy.

Laurence Hays tried not to look as he strolled past with his Jack Russell puppy Bernard. He raised his cap and averted his eyes – Bernard had a quick peep.

'Morning, Mrs Longden.'

'Who was that? Was it Kenneth?'

'No, it was Laurence.'

'That's who I meant. I always get them mixed up – I knew it was somebody of Arabia.'

I tugged and pulled at all sorts of bits and pieces and wondered if my mother was the only person in the world who had ever heard of Kenneth of Arabia and eventually I had her standing upright by the side of the car.

'What Brussels sprout?'

I had to think for a minute. 'The one you made me for the play.'

She twisted the waistline of her skirt round a couple of times until she had the zip centred and then her hands went searching for the hem of her coat which had wrapped itself around the back of her neck.

'You still remember that?'

'It was quite a big day in my life.'

Her head was now down between her ankles, her arms groping up the middle of her back. I could have helped her but I was fascinated.

'I went the next day to watch that play,' she said. 'I didn't say anything at the time – I thought you might be upset.'

'What was it like?'

Her coat was now sitting sniggering on her shoulders and she gave up all hope of ever finding it again.

'The fairies just sat around looking gormless – what was it that it was called?'

'*A Midsummer Night's Dream*.'

'Well, I'll tell you something,' she said as she pushed open the garden gate, 'it could have done with a Brussels sprout.'

I made a pot of coffee while she sorted out her coat in front of the long mirror.

'It was all up around my neck – I'm surprised you didn't notice.'

Whisky was sitting on the step outside the wide-open kitchen door, staring at me as though he were on drugs.

'Come on, then – come on, beauty.'

21

He didn't move. He just sat there staring at a space two inches to the left of my head.

'He won't come in.'

'Course he won't – not with the door open.'

She leant over and slammed the door shut in his face and for a moment or so nothing happened. Then the cat flap quivered and a cat's bottom appeared, followed by two back legs and a tail. There was a pause and then the flap was raised higher and higher as black and white haunches fed themselves piecemeal in through the gap.

Then the body was in and the flap crashed down on the back of Whisky's neck. The bottom shuddered briefly as the shock waves were absorbed and then it continued to reverse. Two front legs, first one black and then one white, stepped in gingerly. Two ears scraped against the lid before flirting into the kitchen and finally a bewildered little face hinged in sideways and Whisky sat down and stared in wonder as the panel snapped shut.

My mother looked on with pride. 'I never thought he'd get the hang of it,' she said, 'he's more intelligent than I thought.'

We drank the coffee in the lounge and over my mother's shoulder I could see two of Diana's small embroideries on the wall. In one there brooded a stark, geometric tree, its desolate branches fingering a moon of gold kid. In the other, the tree was alive and the moon caressed its branches with points of light.

Diana had worked them with her twisted fingers – one for each side of the bed. These two were for us, she said, she had given too many away. My mother had admired them.

'I think they're lovely – very pretty.'

'I'm glad you like them.'

'Of course I'd like them – you are kind. I'll hang

them in the lounge by the French window, they'll go lovely with the carpet. Now are you sure . . . ?'

She was looking at me – polishing the cat's head with one hand and looking at me.

'You're still feeling guilty, aren't you?'

'Yes.'

'You mustn't. Nobody could have cared for her like you did. You loved her – she was always sure of that.'

'I know.'

Guilt has to find its own way out – it can't be dissolved with words. It can't be coaxed out into the open until it's ready – until then it broods deep inside and rots the spirit. Diana had drowned and I had been in the room below – just the floorboards had separated us.

A week ago a man approached me in the street. He listened to me regularly on the radio – he had heard. He put his arm around my shoulder.

'I just wanted to tell you I know how you feel. When I lost my wife it took me a fortnight to get over it.'

I was lucky. I knew what I had lost – but being lucky could be a very painful business.

'He's still got a touch of rheumatism.'

'What?' Her voice filtered in through the walls of my brown study.

'Whisky – he still has the twinges. I told the chemist what you suggested.'

'What I suggested?' An uneasy feeling crept over me and brought me back into the present.

'That I should get him a copper bracelet.'

'Which chemist was this?'

'Betty Brothwoods-as-was.'

I made a mental note and added Betty Brothwoods-as-was to my list of no-go areas.

23

'What did they say?'

'They said there was no demand – not for cats. That's what they always say, isn't it?'

'That's out, then.'

'Looks like it – they hadn't one his size anyway. Come on, Whisky, let's go and give you a bath.'

She picked up the cat and drifted out to the kitchen. I picked up the *Chesterfield Advertiser* and in minutes had drifted off to sleep.

I wasn't sleeping nights. I was still in the bed I had shared with Diana for so many years and with the dark came the memories that haunted me. I tried to programme my dreams – dot them with happy moments as my lids grew heavy. But the black-and-white pictures of times past would become grainy as my brain switched off and then, once more, that final day would burst in on me – in vivid Technicolor.

So I catnapped during the day. A glorious paralysis swept over me. My head floated inches above my shoulders, my arms behaved themselves, my legs were without bones.

I could hear a waterfall in the distance falling gently like a lace curtain, relaxing until it thundered against the rocks below – a wild animal cried out, forlorn and helpless. It was a cat – it was Whisky.

'Come on, Whisky – let's go and give you a bath.'

I staggered to my feet and with my brain on hold, went out to the kitchen.

'What are you doing?'

Whisky was sitting on the draining board, under my mother's restraining hand, staring in some trepidation as the taps roared into the sink. It was foaming up nicely.

'I'm just giving him a wash.'

I sat down on the high stool and watched as my mother tested the temperature of the water and then added just a touch of Domestos to the Fairy Liquid bubbles.

'People don't wash cats.'

'Don't be silly.'

'They don't – they wash dogs and they wash elephants, but they don't wash cats.'

She thought about that for a moment and then said, very thoughtfully, 'I've seen them wash elephants on television – they use a hose-pipe.'

I mustn't put ideas into her head. If she used a hose-pipe on Whisky she'd blast him over the fence and into next door's garden.

'They do it with their tongues – they can get anywhere with their tongues.'

At that moment Whisky chose to illustrate my point by wrapping his left leg round the back of his neck and burying his head in his bottom. He got a quick clip round the earhole for his trouble and looked suitably embarrassed.

'I'm not daft,' said my mother and Whisky gave me a look to see what I thought about that.

'I'm not daft,' she repeated. 'I know most cats can lick themselves clean, but Whisky isn't thorough enough – he doesn't concentrate.'

It was a fair point. Whisky didn't concentrate – it had taken him a year to sort out how that cat flap in the back door worked, and having mastered it in a fashion he had then tried to go out through the letter-box in the front door and got his head stuck. Only quick thinking on the postman's part prevented him from shoving a postcard from Skegness halfway down the cat's throat.

'Anyway,' said my mother, rubbing a handful of soap into Whisky's important little places, 'I'm not washing him, I'm dipping him – you know, like they dip sheep.' And with that she launched him into the sink.

With his white fur plastered flat against his head Whisky bore an uncanny resemblance to Duncan Goodhew, although his breast-stroke left something to be desired and my mother had to keep her hand under his chin to keep him in a straight line.

'Been a blessing this double-draining sink unit,' she said and I couldn't help wondering if the cat shared her opinion. She lifted him out of the foaming mixture at the halfway point and sat him on the narrow divide between the two sinks – he's not a particularly attractive cat at the best of times, today he looked like a dejected ferret.

'They don't like water,' I told her and Whisky gave me a grateful, if somewhat sodden, nod.

'Oh, Whisky does – don't you, love?' and with that she plunged him deep into the rinsing sink.

'You won't find a flea on him,' she declared as she hoisted him out, dripping, on to the far bank. I didn't want to disillusion her, but I had a feeling that the average flea had more intelligence than my mother gave them credit for.

I think she imagined them all panicking like mad, running up and down the decks shouting 'Women and children first', and then leaping screaming into the lifeboats. I'm not too sure about the average lung capacity of the average flea – but I fancy that they could manage to hold their breath for the twenty seconds or so. A good lie-in in the morning and they would be as right as rain.

Meanwhile Whisky was being rubbed down with such vigour that I feared he would emerge from the depths of the towel looking like Duncan Goodhew all over and I hated to think what it was doing to the fleas – especially the children.

His face was a picture of misery and disbelief. 'He didn't like it at first, did you?' She wrung out his tail as though it were a dishcloth.

'He doesn't seem too keen on it now.'

'Oh, he loves it,' she declared and disappeared upstairs to fetch the hairdryer.

Now I must confess, he did seem to enjoy that bit. She blew him dry, combed him out and back-combed him. She did everything except give him streaks and highlights – if he had gone to a hairdresser it would have cost him a fortune. At one point I thought she was going to pluck his eyebrows.

'There – doesn't he look a treat?'

He looked different, I had to admit that. In fact he looked a treat, albeit a rather self-conscious treat. With his fur all fluffed up he stood about three feet across – it was the first time I had seen a cat with an afro.

She plonked him on my knee while she cleared up the kitchen. Then she came and sat in the chair opposite.

'You should see him first thing in a morning when I've just Hoovered him.'

He jumped from my lap and rubbed round her ankles. She picked him up and he sat on her knee and gazed adoringly up at her face and I couldn't help thinking as she stroked her freshly laundered cat, 'It's God help you, son, if ever she buys a tumble dryer.'

Chapter 4

I watched my daughter out on the snowcapped lawn clearing a space for the birds. She was wearing her white Laura Ashley nightdress and my wellingtons – they suited her. Her shovel bit into the drifts and over on the fence a dozen sparrows charted her progress – by her side a robin wearing a black eye patch stood guard and glared fiercely at the sparrows.

'Che Guevara's back,' she yelled.

'Good – he'll be company for you.'

Sally had been devastated by her mother's death, but with a mighty effort of will she and Nick had cushioned me through the rituals and formalities that followed.

Sister and brother had forged a shield of love that protected me and together we had stumbled through from funeral to inquest.

They had sat either side of me in the Buxton courtroom as I stood and answered the coroner's questions, pouring out a story that had bruised my mind a thousand times in the past two months.

The coroner was a kindly man and he had been gentle with me – others in the courtroom had asked questions but they seemed to understand. A verdict was reached: accidental death.

Nick drove the car home to Matlock – I sat in the back with Sally and turned the questions over and over again in my mind. Gradually they took on a sharper edge – they had been designed to peel away layers of my story, to reveal any fragment that didn't fit.

I could see my son's shoulders stiff with indignation as he steered us home. My daughter stared straight ahead, her hands clasped around mine.

'Bastards,' Nick muttered under his breath and the truth hit me like an arrow.

I had never even given it a thought. My children had just sat through a hearing to decide whether or not their father had killed their mother.

I came out of a dream into reality and the shock of it had me sitting bolt upright.

'My God!'

Sally laid her head on my shoulder, her black hair soft against my cheek.

'Never mind, Dad – it's all over now.'

But it wasn't all over for Sally. In a strange way it was harder for her. I discovered Diana's body in the bath – Nick arrived before she had been taken away. It was horrific, but somehow we shared the end with Diana. We had that privilege.

Sally had been two hundred miles away in London – once removed from the tragedy. She heard of it from our lips – when it was all over and done with. Sally had been so close to her mother in life and so far apart in death.

Now the inquest was over and she need be strong no longer. She had protected and comforted me – now she could dissolve into her own private grief.

But she wasn't giving in easily. I sat at the breakfast table and watched her through the window as she tried to make life easy for the birds. Her feathered audience was building nicely – she had a full house this morning and Che Guevara helped her keep them in order until, satisfied with her handiwork, she came in for the bread.

'Have you finished with that?'

I nodded and she plucked the slice of toast from my plate and added it to her collection.

'Pity about the marmalade – they don't like marmalade.'

'I'll remember that in future.'

She sat down at the table and poured a cup of tea that was strong enough for a navvy.

'What are we doing about Christmas? It's only a week away.'

'We could give it a miss.'

'Isn't that being defeatist?'

'Yes.'

'OK then, we'll give it a miss.'

Through the window Che Guevara perched on the spade handle and gestured impatiently at his wrist-watch – stomachs were rumbling out there and he couldn't hold the lads back much longer. Sally sighed and pulled on the wellingtons.

'All right,' she shouted as she pushed open the door. 'Come on, you 'orrible lot, let's be 'aving yew – shortest on the left, tallest on the right. Now move!'

During the first few years of our marriage Diana and I never seemed to get to grips with Christmas. It sort of crept up from behind and mugged us. We worked hard for little money and Christmas Eve would see us trudging home with an anorexic chicken, the runt of the litter, the only one they had left in the shop. By the time it had shrunk from cooking it was able to hide on the plate – skulking behind a convenient sprout. Diana prodded its sad little rump with a fork.

'What do you think – malnutrition?'

'Consumption, more likely.'

Then one day at a party in Chesterfield I met a butcher. He snapped open a cocktail sausage and peered at its soft underbelly. Then he rolled it under his nose like a good cigar and sniffed.

'Crap,' he declared and dropped it into a waste-paper basket. I was impressed and told him about my chickens.

'No problem, I'll put you on my turkey list.' He pulled a book of raffle tickets from his pocket. 'There you are – number seventy-six. Just call in at the shop on Christmas Eve.'

Diana was proud of me when I told her it was all arranged with three months still to go.

'We've got number seventy-six,' I said. 'It's a bit impersonal, isn't it?'

'Perhaps it's better if we don't know his real name,' she told me. 'I wouldn't feel right walking into the shop and telling them I'd come for Norman.'

I was the last customer in the shop that Christmas Eve. The window had been cleared and scrubbed and the few remaining pork pies replaced with a tasteful display of parsley.

'Number seventy-six,' I declared, slapping my ticket on the counter.

A man in a white straw hat examined it carefully and then held it up to the light.

'I think seventy-six has gone,' he said, still staring at the ticket. He turned to a short fat woman at his side. 'Seventy-six – gone, hasn't it?'

'Will have,' she agreed.

He turned the ticket over and examined the back. 'Have we 'owt else?'

'Might have.' She thought.

'What?'

'There's that duck.'

'How many of you is there?' he asked me.

'Two of us.'

'Not be big enough then.'

I could see Diana waiting at the door for me, the hunter home from the hills – and me with an anorexic duck.

31

'What happened to number seventy-six?'

'Oh, it went.'

'How?'

'We sold it – there was only one number seventy-six.' He seemed surprised by the question.

'But I've got the ticket.'

'So I see.'

He picked up an exercise book from the counter and stabbed it with his finger.

'What about that? They'll not be coming for it now.'

The woman took the book off him and thought for a moment.

'It's a bit big, isn't it?'

'He's a growing lad.'

She shrugged and disappeared into the back of the shop. 'Harold,' she shouted into the void, 'give me a hand with this.'

It's a good job I had the van with me, I would never have got the turkey into the car.

'You see,' the man had told me, 'it was supposed to be for a children's home in Alfreton, but they are very unreliable. You can have it for the same price as yours.'

They couldn't find a carrier bag large enough and so I held it close to me and together we waltzed over to the car-park. It would have made two of me – it had thighs like tree trunks and a noble head that rested on my shoulder as we danced.

Diana was wrapping my present when I arrived home and so I wasn't allowed in the kitchen. She always gained full marks for presentation and it could take hours. It was cold outside – I shouted through the door, 'Will you give me a hand to get the turkey out of the van?'

'Why? It is dead, isn't it?'

'Of course it's dead. I wouldn't go within a mile of it if it was alive.'

Together we carried the turkey into the house and laid it on the kitchen table – it dwarfed the sink unit. We each pulled up a chair and Diana, her elbows on the table, her chin in her hands, stared in wonder.

'It still has its head on.'

'I wondered about that.'

'I feel I ought to offer it a drink.'

There was something strange about the bird apart from its size. It rocked from side to side as we talked, a steady motion that didn't wane – it just rocked gently to and fro.

'It's still moving.'

We took a closer look. It was deformed. One breast was that of a weight-lifter, a Schwarzenegger of a breast – the other was a seven-stone weakling. Diana poked it.

'It's deformed.'

'They said it was free-range.'

'Not any more it isn't.'

It was too large to go into the oven and so we ate it bit by bit until it went off in mid-January. It was a relief to have the house to ourselves again, to be able to stretch our legs and not have to speak in whispers.

Out on the lawn Che Guevara was sorting out a bunch of starlings and on the other side of the table Sally sat drying her hair. She looked so much like her mother it was quite unnerving at times.

Yesterday I had fallen on my knees in the hall and opened the post as it clattered through the letter-box. There was a letter from the BBC and I saved that one until last. 'Woman's Hour' had taken six of my short pieces and I raced upstairs to share the good news with Diana – I had pushed open the bedroom door before I remembered that she was no longer there. I

33

turned away and Sally walked out of the bathroom spilling out her pony-tail so that it fell around her shoulders. I had taken a pace towards her, thinking I had been mistaken, before I checked myself.

I watched her across the table as her hair fell down, covering her face. She parted it like a curtain and peered through.

'What?'

'Nothing.'

Can't keep saying 'You reminded me of your mother' – don't want her to think she is a substitute.

'Did I remind you of Mum?'

'Just a bit.'

'Sometimes I look at myself in the mirror and I think she's there. I cried when I saw her first thing this morning.' Sally took her hair in her left hand and brushed stiffly with the right. 'Mum gave me one of her looks and told me not to be so soft.'

I remembered those looks so well. When she had first taken ill I was put in charge of Christmas. Diana issued forth a score of lists and communiqués from her bedroom bunker – there was no doubt that she was still the officer in charge, but now her instructions were being carried out by a rookie.

'Christmas cards – we shall need 200.'

I have always been partial to stage-coaches myself. I think a nice rural scene covered in a foot and a half of snow with a stage-coach pulled up outside a pub and the driver thrashing the horses within an inch of their lives – well, it's what Christmas is all about, isn't it?

But not that year – not with stage-coaches at £1.95 for five and us wanting 200. Even a robin in a woolly hat, sitting on a hollybush with a hot water-bottle under its wing cost 95p for six. It was ridiculous.

So I shopped around a bit. I thought I had made it when I found a stall full at 37p for ten on the market. Granted they were slightly dog-eared and the Wise

Man in the middle looked as though he just travelled forty miles without finding a gents. His camel was slightly blurred and since they were wending their way through what looked like a Norwegian pine forest, it seemed they still had a long way to go before they reached the outskirts of Bethlehem.

I nodded to the man behind the stall, 'Do you have any stage-coaches?'

He shook his head. 'No. Stage-coaches are out this year – this year it's all Wise Men.'

I asked him why that was and he told me that it was because he had 2,500 of the bloody things, that was why.

I still couldn't make up my mind. 'Have you noticed that one of your camels is a bit blurred?'

He studied the card carefully. 'Ah well. What that is, you see – it's your relentless desert sun beating down and reflecting off the desert sand. It does tend to make your camels look a bit hazy, does that.'

'But they're not in a desert – they're in a Norwegian pine forest.'

'Be a mirage, that,' he said. 'Are you having 'em or not?'

'Go on then – I'll have half a dozen.'

'Not at 37p for ten, you won't,' he said. 'It'd take me a fortnight to work it out.'

I made up my mind. 'I'll have ten then – where are the envelopes?'

He was astonished. 'Envelopes? 37p for ten and you want envelopes?'

'Well, it *is* usual.'

'Not here it isn't,' he grumbled. 'Anyway I sold all the envelopes in August. Envelopes sell all the year round – you've got to have a cash flow.'

Diana was sitting up in bed wearing a nightdress that consisted of two thin straps and very little else. My tongue felt as though it had recently been asphalted

35

– she always had this effect on me and I took a sip of her orange juice.

'Have any luck?'

'Yes.'

I plonked the eight boxes of assorted cards on the bed and sat down by her side – high up on the pillow so that I could take full advantage of the view.

'Twenty-five in each – that's 200.'

'You astonish me.'

The newsagent had produced them from under the counter. They were a bargain, he said. 'Left over from last year – if I mix 'em in with this year's lot they'll think there's something funny going on.'

I needed a bargain, at the going rate 200 cards complete with stamps were going to cost me £80 or so.

Diana had the lid off the first box and was examining a card – I examined her nipples.

'What's so Christmassy about a duck sitting on a branch?'

I shook myself out of my day-dream and took the card from her. It was definitely a duck – no it wasn't. 'That's a partridge – it's a partridge in a pear tree, look there's a pear.'

She handed me another. 'There's another pear here – a pair of ducks.'

'No.' I was beginning to get the hang of this. 'They're turtle doves – two turtle doves.' But I had to admit that they definitely had a touch of the mallards about them. The artist seemed to have an obsession with webbed feet.

She quickly flipped through the next two. 'They're all ducks.'

'They can't be.'

'They are – look, there's three ducks on this one and four ducks on that.'

I was into my stride now. 'Those are the three French hens – you can tell, they're wearing berets and those will be the four calling birds.'

'Four calling ducks,' she said with an edge to her voice and I scratched around for a get-out.

'The artist is probably of the primitive school,' I suggested.

'He's a pillock,' she explained.

The next few cards were a distinct improvement. At least they were duckless, there were pipers piping, drummers drumming, lords a'leaping and ladies dancing. The maids a'milking were a little strange, the artist hadn't quite perfected his cows and they were all wearing low-slung rubber gloves.

Diana shuddered. 'Ducks,' she groaned, 'a herd of ducks.'

I stared at the card in her hand and there they were – six geese a'laying. Six little feathered bottoms a'quivering and a'straining.

'Let's open the other box.'

'Let's not.'

But we did and they weren't a bad selection really. There was Santa and his sleigh – I had a quick look to see if his reindeer had webbed feet but fortunately they were up to their knees in snow.

Several cards sprouted holly and one even featured a stage-coach pulling up outside a pub. I relaxed and then Diana said: 'Look at this – is it my eyes or is that camel blurred?'

I watched my daughter as she argued with the robin through the window. She told me he was now demanding a small brown loaf with the crusts cut off as protection money.

It was a cold morning and Sally had devised her own personal central heating system by placing the hair dryer between her feet and pointing it upwards into her nightdress. Very soon she began to swell visibly as though she had thyroid trouble and then, as she turned to wag her finger at the little bird, she slowly deflated and began to look like a woman again.

'Che Guevara didn't wear an eye patch.'

'I know.'

'Then why do you call him Che Guevara?'

'Because he's wearing a beret.'

He was now sitting on the water-butt and swearing violently at the tall kitten from across the road who was taking a short cut through the rockery. He did have a small black beret on his head. I hadn't noticed it before, just the eye patch.

'And if you look very closely you can tell from the bulge under his feathers that he's carrying a gun in a shoulder holster.'

Once again, in Sally's smiling face, I could see Diana.

And, in her words, I could hear my mother. God willing, it was only a phase she was going through.

Chapter 5

So Christmas was a quiet affair. My mother went through the usual charade with her presents – she never bothered to put tags on the parcels. She would hold them to her ear and shake them vigorously, then close her eyes and listen to the ensuing silence.

'That's yours, Nick.'

'Thank you.'

Another shake, another listen and then perhaps a little sniff if she had any doubts.

'Deric.'

'Thank you.'

It takes an experienced glove buyer to tell the difference between a pair of brown leather-type gloves and a pair of black leather-type gloves by just rattling the parcel.

'So that must be yours, Sally.'

'Thank you.'

Sally was prepared to accept the tin of salmon in the spirit in which it had been given, but I suspected something might be wrong. My mother was pleased that I had pointed out the mistake – Whisky would have been disappointed with the powder compact.

When Nick was a little boy he developed a skill not unlike my mother's. For a week or so before Christmas the parcels would build up under the tree until he became almost sick with excitement. He spent hours on his knees squeezing the packages until he developed this talent into a fine art.

He used his forefinger and thumb like a dowser's rod and he could divine an Action Man through two cardboard boxes and a sheet of corrugated paper.

It drove Diana mad and one Christmas she switched the tags on a couple of presents knowing he wouldn't bother with Sally's. We watched from the stairs the next morning as his fingers caressed the parcel and his eyes wondered off in a trance.

It took him a fair time and just when we thought we had him beaten, he snapped back into the real world.

'I think this is yours, Sally, they must have got them mixed up.' He reached out under the tree again. 'Now which one of yours is mine?'

Diana wanted to strangle him but I persuaded her to wait until after Christmas, by which time it had all blown over.

The next year I had a go myself. I wrapped a pound of tomato sausage in two sheets of Christmas paper and laid it amongst the pine needles.

He fumbled with it for the best part of a week and by Christmas morning he wore a frown over his pyjamas as Diana made coffee in the kitchen and I raked out the ashes in the grate.

He knelt down and went straight to work on the sausage, holding the parcel out in front of him as though expecting the Lord to intervene. Diana brought in the coffee just as the fire burst into life and we smiled – fellow conspirators. Then the smiles hit the floor with a thud as we heard him say: 'You know, Sally – I think this is a pound of tomato sausage.'

Diana reached for the poker and as I wrestled with her we heard Sally answer: 'Don't be silly, Nicholas – Daddy wouldn't play a dirty trick like that.'

I never felt so wretched in my life. Daddies shouldn't play around with Christmas, it's too important. This

40

was my favourite time of the year as the children opened their presents, but now I watched with dull eyes.

To make it worse he left the sausage to the last. There was nothing I could do – I couldn't spirit the parcel away from him. He was reading the card out aloud and fiddling with the red ribbon. I had made a good job of wrapping this one.

'Don't expect too much, Nick – it's more of a joke really.'

He smiled at me, a trusting smile, and then the parcel was open and he had the pound of sausage in his hand.

'Thank you.'

'It was a joke, that's all – not a very good joke. I'm sorry.'

'It's all right – it's very nice.'

He looked like a sad little old man as he placed the sausage with his other presents. Sally put her arm around him and gave him a squeeze – a cobra would have been proud of the look she gave me.

Within the week I was forgiven and we kicked a football around on the lawn. Nick was wearing the Derby County football strip which posed as a New Year present, but which we all knew to be a peace offering. He surged into the penalty area, the ball at his feet, threatening my goal.

'How did you know the sausage was tomato?'

He tried to pass me on my left side – he knew it was my weak spot.

'Sally saw you wrapping it up.'

As he wriggled past me, I brought him down from behind with a horrendous tackle and Diana had no hesitation in awarding a penalty – but it was worth it.

My mother loved the pot plants we gave her. We bought her pot plants for every conceivable occasion

41

– birthday, Christmas of course, Mother's Day, Bank Holidays, to celebrate the storming of the Bastille, because it was Tuesday – any day was a good day for pot plants.

'Buy me a plant,' she would say, 'I love plants – you are nearer to God in a garden than you are anywhere where you're not in a garden.'

So we bought her plants. By rights she should have been up to her ears in greenery, hacking her way through from lounge to kitchen. But, entrusted to my mother's care, a pot plant would at first become fretful and then sink into a deep depression before rushing out of the house and hurling itself under a passing bus.

Nick swung the huge hanging basket on to the table and bent down to read the words on the little stick.

'There you are, Nana – it's a Zebrina Pendula.'

'Well, never mind – it looks all right.'

'It needs light.'

'Right – we'll put it near the fire then. Come and have a look at this.'

She led us into the kitchen and pointed to the windowsill where a lonely little hyacinth stood up to its knees in a large pot. It saw my mother coming and it flinched.

'That's the only one left – there were five of them.'

I remembered well enough. Diana had reared them herself from pups and she had given my mother the pick of the litter.

'She can't go wrong with these – she really can't.'

The little hyacinth looked so sad and dejected I wanted to give it a cuddle. The soil was moist, just about right.

'I haven't over-watered it and I give it a quarter-turn every morning, like Diana said.'

There were no draughts from the window and I had exhausted my horticultural knowledge.

'Let's take it home with us,' whispered Sally. 'I shan't sleep if we leave it here.'

My mother poured herself a heaped tablespoonful of Buttercup Syrup and leant against the sink unit.

'I can't understand it – it's only on top that it's not doing very well.'

'Only on top?'

'Yes,' she reached over and took hold of the hyacinth, then she yanked it out of the soil and held the bulb up under my nose, 'just look at the roots on that.'

We all stared at the up-ended plant, its private parts exposed for all to see.

'Do you do that often?'

'Every other day or so – Diana always told me, "Keep an eye on the roots", she said.'

'With everything? Do you do that with everything?'

'Most of them – some are too fiddly.'

I wanted to tell Diana. She had worried for years where she could be going wrong.

'It must be Whisky piddling on them.'

'He can't piddle on every one – no cat could piddle that much.'

'Perhaps he's getting his friends in to help – that cat's never liked me.'

'He hasn't got any friends.'

Diana had thought about it.

'Your mother couldn't be piddling on them, could she?'

The little hyacinth sat on Sally's knee as we drove home and it perked up considerably as she pointed out the nursery where it had been born. Nick had been quite firm about the hanging basket.

'These Zebrina Pendulas, Nana, they have special roots and the daylight mustn't get to them. Don't pull them out whatever you do.'

'Are you sure?'

'Yes.'

43

'They look a lot like those tradescantia I had once
– you had to look at their roots.'

'Well, you don't with these.'

I had given her a kiss over the gate and walked towards the car. I waited while the kids said goodbye.

'What happened to the tradescantia?' I asked her.

'It died. I think Whisky must have piddled on it.'

We watched a lot of television that Christmas. There
was a comedy funeral where the coffin fell out of the
back of the hearse and slid down the hill. The studio
audience seemed to enjoy it, they laughed like a drain
– a year ago I might have laughed myself. Then a
Mafia funeral with wreaths the size of a church door,
a Dracula-type funeral with four black horses pulling
the hearse and a burial at sea.

I had no idea so many people drowned on television.
Often they were young women in the bath – it provides
a good hook early in the first reel. A young woman
naked in the bath, a mysterious stranger on the stairs
and a murder all in the first five minutes. Tension,
drama and bare breasts as the young woman arches
her back in the final death throes. Who the hell is going
to switch channels after a first five minutes like that?

We did – time and time again, only to find on
the other channel a young mother of two dying of
cancer. She hadn't a hair out of place and even her
false eyelashes had miraculously escaped the ravages
of chemotherapy.

Sally kept one eye on the screen, one eye on me
and her trigger finger on the remote-control button.
She switched until we were dizzy – an ominous
chord of music as the heroine stepped into the
shower and Top Cat would come bursting on to
the screen.

We were wary of any film with an expanse of water
in it. Two boys fishing? One might fall in and drown.
Two cowboys fighting in a ford? One might hold the

other's head under water. At least Top Cat usually stayed away from water.

We had an early warning system. The phone would ring and I would hear Nick's stage whisper telling Sally: 'Don't let Dad watch the film on BBC1 tonight – I've seen it.'

Eventually you begin to cope with all this and then it's the small things that catch you unawares.

I pushed the trolley down the supermarket aisle. I always seemed to get the same one – the one with the stiff back left wheel, the one with the will of its own who only ever wanted to go to the cheese counter. It must have been years since it had travelled in a straight line, but with a remarkable show of brute strength I forced it down to fabric softeners and washing-up liquid where it sat and sulked whilst I browsed along the shelves.

I had a '10p off' voucher for Vanish, a new wonder soap that magically removed all stains and probably warts as well. I couldn't find it and so I asked an assistant.

'Have you got any Vanish?'

'No – it's all gone.'

Savouring her answer and filing it away for future use I manhandled the trolley over to toilet rolls – the trolley looked longingly over towards the cheese counter but it knew when it was beaten. It bided its time.

A herd of pink toilet rolls grazed on the top shelf – I can't stand pink toilet rolls, I'm sure God never intended us to wipe our bottoms on pink toilet paper. I looked for the honest-to-goodness white, but it is an endangered species. Six dozen orange occupied the second shelf, slumming it along with the occasional pastel blue. In a dump bin at the far end of the display frolicked a sea of pale green toilet rolls all on offer.

Why is it always the green toilet rolls that are on offer? Why do they make them in the first place if they can't sell the damn things? And where were the white ones?

I spotted a perfect specimen, skulking on the bottom shelf – hiding behind a sprinkling of puffy newcomers all sporting a rather gay daisy motif. They looked suitably embarrassed as I walked on past them so as not to alert my quarry.

Then I knelt down and began stacking the daisy bunch in the aisle.

'Can I help you?' an assistant asked.

'I'm after that one,' I whispered nodding towards the little white roll. He had relaxed and was chatting up the nearest daisy. 'Don't let him see you looking at him.'

The assistant knelt down beside me and helped distract its attention by pretending to tidy up the rubber gloves. I pounced and, grabbing the toilet roll by the scruff of the neck, dragged it screaming out into the open before dropping it feet first into the trolley.

I looked to see if I could find another one – maybe if I had a pair I could breed from them. But no, they are not thick upon the ground these albinos. Another time perhaps.

'That it?' asked the assistant.

'Yes, thank you.'

'Right then.' And she hurried off to the rest-room to tell them, 'He's been in again – that one I told you about.'

Over the fifteen years of enforced domesticity I would have gone mad if I hadn't made a pantomime of it all. Maybe I had gone mad – if so it was quite enjoyable.

We moved on, the trolley and me, down to frozen foods. The little white toilet roll sat up at the front – it was a new world for him and he seemed quite excited.

46

As we eased our way between the cold cabinets towards the ice-cream and assorted puddings I looked around me for something tasty – something different.

I found it. It was a tiny individual apple dumpling sitting all forlorn on the top of a freezer. He was the last one left – all his mates had been sold around him and since he made the freezer look messy he'd been stuck on top until they decided what to do with him.

I picked him up and the tears began to run down my cheeks. Diana used to make such wonderful apple dumplings, huge basin-shaped dumplings, fluffily light, plump with fresh apple and running with juice. For an hour or so I had forgotten all about her.

I had learnt to cope with all those films of people drowning. I could thumb through our photograph albums now without dissolving into tears and only this morning I had sorted through Diana's wardrobe and smiled fondly when I saw the little red hat that she had wanted placed on her coffin.

The wounds were healing – I was on the mend and yet here I was, being mugged in broad daylight by an apple dumpling.

That night in bed I mentally pulled on a pair of cricket pads and went out to bat for England. It usually worked. When the bills were piling up and the taxman hovered, then, as I closed my eyes, Graham Gooch and I would stroll down the steps at Lord's and take on the Australians. We couldn't win the match – we were 695 runs behind, but a draw in this test would seal the series. We needed to bat all day and so as Alderman hurled down the first ball I played a forward defensive stroke with a dead bat.

The second, third and fourth balls would be treated in exactly the same way as would the fifth and sixth. It was so boring that I usually fell asleep halfway through the second over – VAT-man, taxman and bank manager defeated until the morning.

But it wasn't working tonight. Diana was made of sterner stuff and she threaded her way around the edges of my dreams until she took centre stage once more.

She never did much care for cricket and so I turned over and pulled on my football boots, rammed a pair of shin-pads down my socks and ran out on to the lush turf of Wembley. The crowd went wild.

Chapter 6

Roy MacFarland provided me with the perfect through ball – the Manchester United defence stood still and appealed for offside, but the referee waved me on and as the goalkeeper advanced to the six-yard line, a hundred thousand spectators held their breath as I chipped the ball high over his head and into the far corner of the net.

I stood back modestly to let the rest of the Derby County team climb the famous Wembley steps and then, to thunderous applause, I hauled my weary body up to meet the Queen.

She winced as she caught sight of the blood-soaked sponge I held against my head and then, as she handed me my medal, a phone rang by her side.

'It's for you,' she said, 'it's your mother.'

Nobody answered when I spoke into the alarm clock, so I wriggled over to the other side of the bed and picked up the phone instead.

'Hullo.'

Nothing – the Queen had been right, it was definitely my mother. She would have gone to feed the cat or emulsion the back bedroom or something. For some reason she had the idea that dialling took ages – gearwheels had to grind into action, pulleys would be brought into play, points had to be shifted into place by heavily muscled engineers. So no point in wasting time while all this went on – she might as well do something useful.

'Hullo – Mum?'

At least it gave me time to wake up. I peered across at the two alarm clocks sitting side by side on the bedside table and then, as I shut one eye, they slowly merged into one – seven fifteen on a Sunday morning.

'Are you there, Mum?'

Of course she wasn't – she'd probably decided to do a little light ironing or concrete the garden path.

The bedroom door opened and a crumpled Sally shuffled in. She blinked at the table lamp and then curled up into a ball on the end of the bed.

'Who is it?'

'Nobody's answered yet.'

'Give her my love.'

I lit a cigarette and waited. Down the phone I could hear her moving across the hall, talking to Whisky.

'Don't do that – I haven't had that carpet long. Stop it. Do you know how much that carpet cost? It was from Eyres, it's Axminster – they're expensive, it cost over £300 what with the fitting. I've got the invoice somewhere – I think it's in the desk in the back bedroom.'

I heard her footsteps as she climbed the stairs. Sally stretched and then rolled up again.

'Isn't she there yet?'

'No – she's just gone upstairs to show the cat an invoice.'

I must have nodded off for a moment and then I was jerked awake by a voice.

'Hello – is anybody there?'

'Mum?'

'Oh good – it's worked.'

I was always at a disadvantage during these early morning calls, partly because the daylight had yet to enter my soul, but mainly because my mother wrote the script.

'I just wanted to tell you that I've bought a house.'

50

'But you've got a house.' And one she always said she would leave only when Hattersley's men carried her out feet first.

'Oh, I'm selling this one – I've just rung the estate agent.'

'You've just rung the estate agent? At a quarter past seven on a Sunday morning?'

'He wasn't at his office, so I rang him at home. It's all right, they have to be up early – they've got a Shetland pony.'

I had coffee and a slice of toast with Sally before setting off for Chesterfield.

'I won't be long.'

'Why has Nana bought a Shetland pony?'

'I'll explain it all to you when I get back.'

My mother explained it all to me and for the first time in a long time her story made some sort of sense. The garden was getting too big for her, she said, she could handle it at the moment, but when the day came that she couldn't, the right house wouldn't be available – as it was, she'd seen this place just round the corner and it was perfect. She would still be near her friends.

'Kitty's house – you remember Kitty. Well, her son came to see me and asked me what it was worth, he said he was thinking of asking £16,500. I told him it was worth £19,000 of anyone's money – I'd give him that.'

And she had. She'd gazumped herself by £2,500 in a split second.

I didn't bat an eyelid. I waited until I had told Sally about it and then we both cried together.

We wondered how she would cope with a string of would-be buyers trooping through her house and so I arranged for the sale board to read, 'By Appointment Only'. Then in theory I could arrange to be there.

In practice a couple would knock at the door and ask if they could have a look round.

'I'm very sorry. Viewing is by appointment only.'

'When would be convenient then?'

'You can have a look round now if you like.'

She adopted a rather unusual selling technique. She insisted on showing everyone the damp patch behind the hall cupboard the moment they put their heads round the door – she would point out the total lack of central heating and then confuse the issue by claiming that the solid-fuel boiler in the kitchen was capable of running thirty-seven radiators. I had never heard this one before, but she insisted that it was true because the Irishman who had asphalted the drive had said that his mother had one just like it.

She told all and sundry that the entire house needed rewiring and to prove her point made them switch on the light in the pantry, which resulted in each and every one of them getting a violent electric shock that hurled them back into the kitchen.

This selling-in-reverse technique had a strange effect on her potential customers. 'Yes,' they would say after she had pointed out that the letter-box would have your fingers off if you weren't careful, 'but what about that oak panelling in the hall? And the brick fireplace – that's fantastic. I've never seen another one like it in my life.'

'And you're hardly likely to,' she would tell them, 'my husband built it and he never could use a plumb line.'

Then she would make them lie down with her on the hearthrug whilst she pointed out where it was beginning to crack and how it wasn't quite in line with the chimney breast.

'Now come and have a look at the plumbing in the bathroom – talk about Heath Robinson.'

And off they would troop up the stairs, my mother picking up the Vim on the way so that she could show them how impossible it was to remove the green stain from the wash-basin.

'I've fixed up some appointments-only,' she told me on the phone later that morning, 'for half past five tomorrow.'

'Some?'

'There's six couples coming and a widower from North Wingfield – I've bought some iced buns from Henstocks and I've ordered an extra pint.'

'They're all coming at half past five?'

'The widower might be late – he has his mother to think about.'

The journey back from Manchester took longer than I had anticipated – I rang her from Chapel-en-le-Frith.

'That's all right, don't worry – they seem to be enjoying themselves.'

The first couple had arrived at dead on five and been given the special inclusive tour which took in the faulty handle on the back bedroom door.

'Go in there.'

'Right.'

'Now try and get out.'

The second couple had followed hard on the heels of the first and waited patiently in the kitchen.

'Put the kettle on, love, I won't be a minute.'

By the time I arrived the party was in full swing. My mother was on the settee with her feet up, an iced bun in one hand, a sweet sherry in the other.

'Would you like a sherry?' a lady with a tray and a small moustache asked me.

'No, thank you.'

'There's another bottle in the coal bucket.'

A man with a much larger moustache put his head round the French window.

'You must have a couple of hundred roses out here, Mrs Longden – will you be leaving them?'

'Might as well – they're covered in greenfly.'

The doorbell rang. 'You sit there,' said the lady with the moustache, 'I'll show them round.' My mother sank back on to the settee.

'She's been a real treasure, I don't know what I would have done without her – they arrived first.'

A lady I hadn't seen before came in out of the garden and asked if she could show me round the house and then the lady with the moustache hurried back downstairs. 'Forgot to take the Vim with me,' she explained.

The party broke up at about half past nine. The widower from North Wingfield was the first to go – he had his mother to think about and so he missed the bit where my mother demonstrated how difficult it was to light the gas fire. The male half of couple number two said he was a fitter with the gas board and he would pop in tomorrow, 'unofficial-like', and fix it for her. There was a distinct rumbling among the others who seemed to think that this was taking an unfair advantage and, just when I half expected someone to propose that we all meet again next year, the fraternal spirit that had flowered during the evening withered slightly and no-one promised to write.

I washed the dishes and my mother dried. She flicked the lid of the breadbin with her foot and Whisky staggered out into the light.

'I hope he settles – I've heard of cats walking 500 miles back to their old homes.'

'You're only going 400 yards down the road – he'll hardly have to jump on a tramp steamer.'

'He won't know any cats on Storrs Road.'

'He doesn't know any cats here – he never goes out.'

As though to prove me wrong Whisky strolled over to the cat flap and stuck his head through, then changed his mind – it was dark.

'I think I'll take that with me.'

'What?'

'The cat flap.'

'You can't do that – it'll leave a hole in the door.'

'I suppose so. Still – it'd be handy for the new people if they had a cat and wanted to put a cat flap in, wouldn't it? Be ready made.'

We drank coffee at the old oak table my father had made – it was beginning to warp at one end, but somehow it looked all the better for it. We had spent many hours around this table – Sally and Nick would bring their hard-earned pocket-money pennies in little pot pigs and lose them to my mother playing Newmarket. Miraculously, and against all odds, they would win the final hand and carry home their pigs stuffed with silver.

I remembered the moment when I saw the gap between my father and myself widen so that it could never be bridged – a little thing in itself.

He was sitting at that end of the table, over there, the end near the fire. My mother wasn't allowed to have the paper until he had finished with it – she messed it up – so he read it slowly.

When, at last, he put the paper down, he folded it neatly and we waited for the day's pronouncement on the world in general.

'You know,' he said, picking up the paper again as my mother reached for it, 'I can't understand why

55

Freddie Mills would commit suicide – he can't have been short of a bob or two.'

I knew then that I would never reach him and the last thread of love I had for him snapped – he could manage without my love, he would never be short of a bob or two.

'Don't be too hard on him.'

'On who?'

'Your dad.'

'How did you know . . . '

'You get that look about you. He made this table, you know. Built to last, he said – it's coming apart at that end, have you noticed?'

'Yes.'

'I shan't be sorry to get away from here. Be the final break – he won't be around any more. Everything he touched came apart in the end – even you and me.'

It was the most profound remark I had ever heard my mother make – I didn't quite understand it, but I was most impressed.

'How do you think it went tonight?' she asked.

I thought it had been a total disaster. Tomorrow I would ask the estate agent to channel all the enquiries through me.

'I thought it went very well,' she said.

'So did I.'

'Let's have another sherry then – I hid a spare bottle in the coal bucket.' She walked over to the fireplace. 'My God – it's gone. Still, never mind – it was a good investment, wasn't it?'

She was going to be so disappointed when nothing came of the evening. I couldn't see a genuine buyer amongst the lot of them.

The next morning the estate agent rang me. Every one of them had made an offer, with the exception of the widower from North Wingfield, that is – but then he had his mother to think about.

'We'll keep it on the market though – I think we can do better.'

'Fair enough.'

'She's a remarkable woman, your mother. Do you know she rang me at home, on a Sunday morning, just after seven o'clock?'

'Yes, I'm sorry about that.'

'She was as bright as a button.'

'She said you had to be up early to feed the Shetland pony.'

'Did she?'

'You haven't got a Shetland pony, have you?'

'No – pity really, but they'd never let me keep one in the flat.'

Chapter 7

I opened the knife drawer and took out my toothbrush. The face flannel was in a plastic bag by the teaspoons, but the toothpaste and soap had made a pathetic break for freedom and were hiding behind the garlic crusher at the back.

I couldn't go on like this. The sink was full of dishes from last night. The remains of Sally's Weetabix had set like concrete and a buttered-toast soldier stood at ease, resting against the cold tap.

The milk pan was catching forty winks on the windowsill, taking advantage of the pale winter sun and it dozed on as I held it under the tap. It awoke with a start as the jet of water struck the business end of a spoon lying half submerged in a quarter of an inch of milk.

The result was electrifying. The front of my shirt was soaked by the redirected jet. The milk pan hurled itself bodily at a wine glass and the toast soldier crumpled and fell lifeless into the sink. I couldn't go on like this.

I hadn't been in the bathroom since Diana drowned – I couldn't face it. Once or twice I had steeled myself and reached for the door handle, but then my nerve had cracked and I had quickly walked away.

The memory of that day was still raw. I only had to close my eyes and I could see her lying face down in the bath, her hair streaming on the surface of the water. I didn't need to go into the bathroom to see her lying on the floor beneath me as I made a pitiful attempt to bring her back to life.

I could see her now as I cleared the debris from the sink, stripped off my soaking shirt and spread my toothpaste on my brush.

For weeks now I had toured the shower cubicles of Matlock on a carefully planned schedule so as not to inconvenience my friends. They had welcomed me with open arms but it would begin to pall eventually as I grew old and infirm.

I must sell the house of course and get away – make a new start. But until then . . .

I gathered up soap, flannel and razor and screwed the top back on the toothpaste. Do it now – right now. Don't think about it.

At the foot of the stairs I began to sing very loudly. As a child I could drive away ghosts if I sang very loudly. Nowadays, on long car journeys, I kept my worries at bay in a cracked baritone and as long as the windows were tight shut and the sun-roof closed it seemed to work. I must be a very strange person.

'She was poor but she was honest, Victim of a rich man's game. First he loved her, then he left her, And she lost her maiden name . . . It's the same the whole world over, It's the poor wot gets the blame, It's the rich wot gets the gravy. Ain't it all a bleedin' shame?'

Where the hell had I dragged that one from? Not a bad attempt really except that I had sung it to the tune of 'Old Man River'.

The bathroom door was ahead of me. Now the handle was in my hand and I was in. The sink straight in front of me, the bath to my right – don't look at the bath.

I brushed my teeth – twice, then trimmed my beard and shaved my neck very slowly. I must stay in as long as possible, until I had conquered the dread.

Nothing more to do now unless I cleaned my teeth once more. I forced myself to turn and face the bath. Would I ever be able to climb in there again?

I leant over and turned on the taps and then, after pushing the plug in place, sat on the stool and waited. Diana would have sat here waiting for me to come and help take off her nightdress and then lift her into the water.

But I had been busy downstairs struggling with a temperamental washing-machine. If only I had packed it properly the first time – if only.

I stood up. She would have been tired of waiting – tried to take the nightdress off. She couldn't do that, couldn't lift her arms above her head. So she would try to wriggle out of it and then when it got stuck around her knees, maybe she tried to stand, overbalancing and then . . .

The water had reached the overflow now and I turned off the taps. Slowly I undressed and then, naked, I sat on the stool again. It was now or never.

It was to be never. I pulled out the plug and watched the water rush until it began to spin. Then I walked downstairs, through into the kitchen and kicked the washing-machine very hard.

Then I put my shoes on and kicked it once again.

Sally was still with me. She had a good job at the Park Lane Casino in London but she couldn't face it yet – her emotions were too brittle, she would burst into tears without warning and that would never do at the blackjack tables. They were being very patient and waited to hear from her.

'So let's put the house up for sale.'

'I shall have to find somewhere else first.'

And that wasn't going to be easy. I should be moving for the sake of moving. Simply to get away. Not to be where I wanted to be but just to find a safe house – a sterile unit where I could lick my wounds for a time.

The fact was – I wasn't well. The fifteen years of caring had taken their toll. I was down to a pound under eight stone from ten and a half, completely exhausted, and both mentally and emotionally I wasn't fit for the blackjack tables either.

'You could stay with Nana until you find a place you like – think about it.'

She watched my face as I thought about it and changed her mind. 'No, don't think about it.'

I didn't think about it. It didn't bear thinking about.

There was another problem. I had a living to earn. I was supposed to be a humorist and I didn't feel like turning up for work right now.

Editors and producers were giving me a breather. They weren't going to ring up and say, 'Sorry about your wife, Deric – could you let me have a funny piece on the January sales?'

They were decent people and they would wait for me to ring them. Of course there's always the exception to the rule and this time it was Ashley Franklin of Radio Derby.

Ashley paid me peanuts. BBC local radio producers weave programmes out of thin air, their currency being fragile promises, faint praise and a brand of foul coffee that has more than a hint of Nitromors about it. They do an impossible job and most of them do it very well indeed. Ashley was one of the best although I would never dream of telling him so, he was insufferable as it was.

His voice, which is much taller than he is, forced itself down the line in an attempt to beat the background babble in the studio.

'Deric – how do you fancy doing a piece for Friday morning?'

'I don't.'

'Good. You can take your choice. We've got an item on the best time to have your cat doctored and then there's a phone-in on do-it-yourself.'

I thought about it. 'Will people want to do it themselves, Ashley?' I asked him. 'From all accounts it's rather a messy business – isn't it perhaps better to leave it to the vet?'

'I think you've got hold of the wrong end of the stick.'

'There you are, you see. If I can't even get hold of the right end of the stick, then I'm certainly better off leaving it to the vet.'

'The do-it-yourself sequence is on cavity wall insulation. You bore a hole and pump in thousands of bubbles through a nozzle.'

'It sounds a bit rough on the cat, Ashley. Are you sure he's a proper vet?'

I enjoyed my conversations with Ashley Franklin. He always let me win unless he was feeling stroppy and today he was being easy on me and trying to nurse me back to work.

'Half past ten on Friday then – you've got it half written already.'

Good old Ashley. It would give me something to work on and then, of course, there was always the money – I'd be able to pay the milkman.

I pulled the car to a halt outside Nick's house and watched as my daughter-in-law Jo attacked a small tree in the front garden. It must have done something awful to deserve such treatment. She saw me coming.

'Hi.'

'Hullo, love – what did it do, answer you back?'

'I'm training it.'

She glared at the little tree and it trembled.

'Nick playing football?'

'No – he's doing some jobs in the house.'

She must be training Nick as well. He had never done any jobs at home. Through the window I could see a pair of jeans, the knees were just about level with my eyes.

'He's grown, hasn't he?'

'He's standing on a stool.'

I pushed open the front door and went in to witness this miracle for myself. Nick was drilling a row of neat holes with his Black and Decker, man and machine in perfect harmony, both of them trying hard to give the impression that they were grown up.

I stared at him open-mouthed. Where had he learnt these skills? Certainly not at home. Only a year earlier he had asked me to fit a three-pin plug to his stereo unit and swore blind that he had never seen a three-pin plug before in his life.

The pelmet matched the holes perfectly and Nick climbed down from his stool.

'Been handy this drill. I've put up the clock and three shelves in the kitchen. Fixed the bathroom cabinet to the wall, that mirror in the back bedroom and now that's all the pelmets done.'

'Who put the three-pin plug on the drill for you?' I wanted to know, but he smiled that slow smile of his and patted me on the head.

'Want a cup of tea?' he asked me and we drifted into the kitchen. Jo joined us and sat with me at the brand-new pine table. I had told them that it would be too large for their small kitchen. It fitted perfectly.

'He's never had that drill out of his hand,' she whispered. 'I bet he stirs his tea with it.'

Nick filled the kettle with water and switched it on, displaying yet another hitherto unsuspected talent.

'Do you know you're wearing one black glove and one brown glove?' he asked me.

'Yes.'

'That's all right then.'

He sat down with us and Jo played mother.

Every year for as long as I could remember my mother bought me a pair of gloves at Christmas, and every year one of them would make a break for it within the week.

I still had the left-hand partner of the brown pair she bought me for my birthday in November. It had lain pining in a drawer ever since the right hand had gone walkabout later that day. But now I was able to introduce it to the remaining black Christmas glove and once again my hands were swathed in plastic.

Nick was even better than I was at losing gloves. One Christmas he unwrapped a pair, kissed my mother and put them down on the carpet and we never saw them again.

We had a running competition to see who could get most excited as we opened my mother's loosely wrapped parcels. On his twentieth birthday he drooled as he tore at the string and then stared in bewilderment. There was only one glove in the parcel – he'd lost it before he'd even got it. We mentioned it to my mother but she didn't seem to understand what all the fuss was about.

Nick was sure to have lost one already – we could toss up to see who got the matching pair.

'I've still got mine. They're in the car – in the glove compartment.'

I couldn't believe it. Not only did he still have both gloves, but he was filing them in the right place. I'd never met anyone before who kept gloves in a glove compartment.

And this was the kid who once lost so many mittens that Diana tied a piece of string to each one so that it went up one sleeve, across his shoulder and down the other sleeve. When he came home that night he still had the mittens, but he'd lost the piece of string.

'Right,' said Jo. 'I'll get back to my tree.' Poor little sod – it had probably never harmed anyone in its life.

Nick leant back on his chair and stretched. He poured me a second cup of tea.

'How's it going?'

'Fine.'

'Are you working?'

'I've a piece to do for Ashley.'

'That's it?'

'Yes.'

'It's not enough.'

He had that look in his eye that told me he was about to take charge.

When he was little we would go out for the day together and stop for a meal. He had such an appetite that I often feared he was about to start on the place mats, whilst I just stared at my plate and shuffled the food about. We would order for one grown-up and a child's portion – when the waiter had disappeared we would swop plates. I could sense the role-reversal coming. My son, the father-figure.

'You need something to get your teeth into.'

'Yes.'

'What about that television thing you started with Aileen?'

'I couldn't handle that – not yet.'

'The Television Thing' was to be a play about a disabled woman – a story that closely mirrored Diana's running battle with pain and frustration. I had the title and the music – both would be 'Wide Eyed and Legless' – and there was a basic storyline that I had mapped out in harness with novelist Aileen Armitage. But I wasn't ready for it yet – it was too soon.

'It hurts too much at the moment.'

'That's why it might be a good time to write it.'

'No.'

He came in at me from a different angle – this time from out of the sun.

'So what are you doing for Ashley?'

'Just a five-minute piece – about taking the cat to be doctored . . . ' I tailed off – it sounded ridiculous. 'I've got to come to terms with everything first, Nick – I can't spend the next twelve months going over all that again.'

'Isn't that what you're doing anyway?'

'I suppose so.'

'Well then?'

It was asking too much. At least there were times now when I could forget for a while.

'I'll think about it.'

As I coaxed the car up the steep hills leading out of Two Dales my hands felt cold on the steering-wheel. I had left my gloves on Nick's kitchen table. Perhaps right now he would be drilling two little holes with his Black and Decker, one in each glove, so that a piece of string could go right up one sleeve, across my shoulders and down the other.

Chapter 8

The removal van stood outside my mother's new headquarters in Storrs Road – it seemed a different shape than it had been when Nick hired it first thing this morning. He walked around it, poking the bulges in the sides.

'What am I going to tell them?'

'Always tell the truth,' said my mother. 'That's what I always say.'

'They'll think I'm an idiot.'

'Then make something up.'

Nick opened the rear doors with some difficulty. They bowed outwards to meet him and the clasp was bent. He jumped inside and we watched as he examined the damage.

'What am I going to say?'

I thought I might be able to help. 'Tell them that you ignored your father's advice, even though he always knows best, and drove for three quarters of a mile with a loose garden roller in the back.'

'I can't tell them that.'

'It's what happened.'

'I know – but I can't tell them that.'

My mother found the adjustable step and climbed aboard.

'There's a lot more room in it now than there was before,' she told him but the fact didn't seem to lift his spirits.

The roller slumped exhausted in the far corner of the van, its handle drooping along the floor as my mother searched around for the few bits and pieces that had accompanied it on that last trip of the day.

She gave a cry of triumph and emerged carrying her Lloyd-Loom linen basket. It was as flat as a dartboard and she had it tucked under her arm.

'They're coming back in, are these,' she declared, 'they're asking a fortune for them.'

'I'll buy you another one,' said Nick miserably.

'Oh no you won't – I was fed up with it anyway.'

I reached to take it from her.

'Give it to me, I'll stick it out by the dustbins.'

'No.' She clutched it to her chest and marched off down the path. 'I put three lampshades, the spare kettle and some teabags inside it – they might be all right.'

The teabags survived and we sat in her new lounge and sampled a couple of them. Nick had gone to take the van back and Sally was riding shotgun to make sure he didn't get lynched.

It was a pleasant little house. It didn't have the character of the one she had left but my mother would soon change that.

'I think I can settle here,' she said. 'Whisky seems to have settled already.'

There was some truth in that statement. Whisky was fast asleep in his breadbin. It was a roll-top model that he had inherited from my mother and he had adopted it as his sleeping quarters. He had been having forty winks in there when Sally picked it up in the old house and placed it in the back of the removal van. He slept on as Nick carried the breadbin into the new house and set it down on the hearthrug. He was still in there now, snoring his head off, totally unaware that anything had happened.

It was half past five. In exactly 27 minutes the little alarm clock in his head would go off and he would bang on the inside of the roll-top lid waiting to be let out for his tea.

My mother poured herself two fingers of Buttercup Syrup into a tablespoon and smacked her lips.

'He should be all right – he's very easygoing.'

I must admit that I had never thought of Whisky as easy-going. Paranoid, neurotic and schizophrenic? Yes. But easygoing? Never.

He had been just a small bundle of fluff when the RSPCA found him huddled up in a cardboard box on the M1. He had obviously been thrown from a car and was a very disturbed kitten indeed.

The RSPCA wanted to place this disturbed kitten in a house where his behaviour would go almost unnoticed and naturally they thought of my mother.

For the first week of his new life he sat on the electricity meter in the pantry facing the wall.

'He's shy,' my mother told us, 'he's been very frightened and he doesn't want to talk about it.'

She fed him on the meter, placing little bowls of milk and fish under his nose. Every now and then she would lift the kitten in the air and place an old baking tray spread with sand under his bottom. The kitten could perform on cue and within a minute or so the tray would be shuffled out from underneath him leaving him free to continue his vigil, still facing the wall.

One morning he strolled out of the pantry and took up residence in a Morland fur-lined boot. He came out twice a day to eat but wouldn't even glance at anyone who happened to be in the vicinity.

Whenever he wanted to use the baking tray he would simply squat in the middle of the kitchen, staring at the floor, and wait to be lifted so that the tray could be eased into position.

Then one day he found his pipe-cleaner and it changed his life. We never knew where it came from – nobody in the house smoked a pipe, but as I chatted to my mother, each of us in a fireside chair, the little kitten left his fur boot and joined us on the hearthrug, the pipe-cleaner sticking at a jaunty angle from his mouth as he gazed into the flames.

Since then it had been with him at all times. It was his comfort blanket, status symbol and executive toy all rolled into one. Whenever he went out he would leave it by the door and then pick it up again the moment he came back in. He would have it with him now in the breadbin.

My mother held her bottle of Buttercup Syrup up to the light. It was empty. She seemed to get through gallons of the stuff.

'I shouldn't drink too much of that if I were you.'

She turned the bottle upside down and pushed it up inside the belly of the shade over the table lamp.

'It's good for you.'

There was a loud twang as she clicked it in between two of the wire struts and then, with a twist of the wrist, she jammed it into place and withdrew her empty hand leaving the bottle dangling.

'There – it's been handy, has this.'

She held an expectant spoon immediately under the neck of the bottle and waited for the first dribble. 'I only have a heaped tablespoonful.'

'Yes but how many?'

'Just the one at a time.'

A thin trickle of syrup reached the spoon and, having now worked out the trajectory, she gently lowered the spoon until it rested on the table, the syrup falling eighteen inches in an intermittent flow.

'There you are.' She sat back in her chair and glowed with pleasure.

'It's very easy to become addicted,' I began, 'too much of anything can be . . . ' But she wasn't interested in listening to boring people. She stood up.

'Come with me – I want to show you something.'

I waited whilst she sampled the first fruits from her distillery and then, with an appreciative purr, she placed the spoon back in the firing line and led me upstairs to the little back bedroom.

She had spent most of the day in there whilst the kids and I had ferried her heavy oak furniture into the house. If she couldn't help, she couldn't bear to watch.

She paused, her fingers on the doorhandle. For a moment I thought she was going to declare the back bedroom well and truly open.

'Close your eyes.'

I closed my eyes and heard the door creak as she pushed against it.

'You can look now.'

Aladdin's mouth would have watered – but only for a split second or so. Spread around the room was her collection of Crown Derby, Royal Doulton, Coalport and Wedgwood. An embroidered Victorian fire screen stood guard in the corner and on the windowsill rested nine busts depicting William Shakespeare in a variety of moods ranging from stolid to impassive.

Her silver bits and pieces graced a small table in company with an eighteen-piece dinner-service. It was now in roughly forty-three pieces.

'I've put all my treasures together. Those are my favourites – the Crown Derby.'

She moved forward to pick up a little shepherd boy and his head dropped off.

'It does that,' said my mother.

The head rolled across the table and came to rest at the feet of an elegant Regency buck who was looking backwards over his left shoulder at a sheep being chased by a sheep-dog; it had no need to worry, the dog had only three legs and would never catch it.

A matchstick poked out of the shepherd boy's neck and as I picked up his head and leant my weight on the

71

table to restore him to his former glory, the buck took his eyes off the sheep and his head slowly swivelled round to see what I was up to.

On closer inspection I could see that the worried-looking sheep had his front near-side leg glued in place – the fact that the limb was that of some other animal gave him a rather lop-sided look and it gave me a clue as to why the dog was chasing him. It was his leg.

One by one I picked up the china figures. Each of them had done battle with my mother and lost. In her Florence Nightingale role she must have got through the best part of a box of Swan Vestas as neck after fragile neck had been fractured.

Heads turned away on their matchsticks and were humbly bowed as though the figures were ashamed of themselves. A fine bone-china cavalier was the only non-amputee amongst the lot of them.

'Do you think they're worth anything?' asked my mother.

I thought that Robert Brothers' Circus might be persuaded to make a bid.

'I've got some more in that box over there,' she told me, 'but they're broken.'

I moved on to the silver – she couldn't break silver. I picked up an antique teapot and the lid came away with the hinges.

'That's loose,' she said. 'Have you seen this? This is lovely.'

The embroidered fire screen had its back to us. It had belonged to her grandmother and was thankfully still in one piece. I turned it round to face us. She had set fire to it.

'I'm clumsy, aren't I?'

She was forever picking up her treasures to touch them, to feel the quality of a lovely piece in her hand. She would take a figure with her into the kitchen whilst she washed the dishes, standing it on the draining-board so that she could appreciate it as she worked. Then a misdirected flick with the tea-towel or a jutting elbow would send it spinning and it was time for the Swan Vestas again.

She held the nodding-head shepherd boy in her hand and fondly stroked his shirt buttons with her thumb.

'I still see them as they were when I bought them. I get just as much pleasure from them now – more in fact, because they're friends really.'

So what the hell. That's what it's all about, I suppose – a reasonable alternative to being preserved behind glass for fifty years simply in order to make a guest appearance on some future 'Antiques Road Show'.

All the same it hurt. My heritage was being paraded before me and it had a matchstick poking out of its neck. I picked up the cavalier who seemed to be the sole survivor of the carnage.

'I think this is all right.'

'Let's take it downstairs,' she suggested, 'the electricity's weak in this bedroom – it has to come uphill.'

In the lounge I set the figure down on the mantelpiece, under a wall light. He obviously had a better doctor than the others, perhaps he had gone private – he was 3 per cent bone china and 97 per cent Bostik.

My mother eased herself into her chair and taking the cavalier from me she placed it precariously on the arm. It rocked gently from side to side as she leant over to assess the Buttercup Syrup situation.

It was non-ongoing. The trickle had stopped but the spoon was piled high with a fat belly of syrup. In slow motion, and with the steady hand of a twenty year old, she brought it to her lips and then her tongue flicked out to finish the job. She sat back in her chair, at peace with the world, as she caressed the cavalier on her knee.

'See what I mean – it's much brighter down here.'

'You have 150-watt bulbs down here and only a 40-watt bulb in the bedroom.'

'I see,' she said, 'and you think that might have something to do with it, do you?'

Sally and Nick returned just in time to see Whisky emerge from the breadbin. The lid rattled as he stirred and Sally whipped it up so that he could have a good look at his new home. We waited – Whisky is a cat who likes to take his time.

He stretched, first the front paws, chin on the rug, bum in the air and then the rear paws, back arched, bum on the ground – he nodded to us and picked up his pipe-cleaner, then set off to the kitchen for a light snack.

Only he couldn't find it. He looked everywhere but somebody had moved the kitchen. He sat staring at a wall where once he remembered there had been a door. My mother picked him up.

'Come on, love, I'll give you a tour.'

They disappeared out into the hall, Whisky staring back over her shoulder, his pipe-cleaner drooping, a look of pure disbelief on his face. I had a stretch myself, it was time to be off.

'We'd better get home,' said Sally, 'so you can get some work done.'

'I suppose so.' What did she have in mind?

'You'll have some writing to do, won't you?'

'I've just got a small piece to finish. For Ashley.'

'Oh?' She was terribly interested. 'What's that about then?'

I glanced at Nick. He was counting the cracks on the cavalier. I could sense a conspiracy. She knew damn well what it was about.

'It's about having your cat doctored.'

'And is that it?'

'Yes.'

74

She nodded and tried to catch Nick's eye for support. He was examining the table lamp and wondering why a Buttercup Syrup bottle should be stuck up a lampshade. She was on her own.

'Nick and I have been talking.'

'I thought you might have been.'

'We think you ought to concentrate on the television play. Do something worthwhile – it would be good for you.'

'Maybe I will, one day.'

'Have a talk with Aileen about it.'

'I might do that – when I'm ready.'

'Tomorrow?'

My mother saved me, God bless her. She sailed into the room with Whisky tucked under her arm.

'Whisky thinks it's very nice here.'

'Good.'

'He's had a wee in his cat litter.'

The cat grinned at us as though expecting a round of applause and seemed disappointed when we got up to go.

He hung in mid-air under my mother's arm as she stood at the door to see us off and wondered what else he could do to impress us.

We piled into the car and as I turned the key in the ignition we waved goodbye. My mother gave us a lovely smile and as she flung her arm high into the air to wave back – the cat dropped with a dull thud on to the concrete path.

I made a mental note to have a close look at Whisky the next time I called. He would probably have a matchstick poking out of his neck.

Chapter 9

The tall kitten from across the road watched as I opened the garage door. Last week the up-and-over door had gone up and over and off and the tall kitten had sat on the fence and smirked behind his paw as the huge wooden frame crashed down on to the roof of the Citroën.

He was in the front row again and this time he had a small ginger friend with him. Word had got around that here was a show not to be missed, but this time they were disappointed.

I eased it gently overhead and although the concrete weights groaned and the wires screamed in terror, the huge door behaved impeccably as it tucked itself in under the flat roof. Out of the corner of my eye I could see the tall kitten apologizing to his friend.

The Citroën was pleased to see me and wagged its exhaust-pipe in greeting – I must get that fixed, in fact the whole car was well past its sell-by date and, judging from the pool of oil on the garage floor, it had haemorrhaged during the night.

But it bounced along happily enough as we skirted Sheffield and headed for the M1, the arthritic rattle of the dashboard being mercifully drowned by a deep-throated roar from the shattered exhaust. The radio reception was also less than perfect, which surprised me – that was a brand-new wire coat hanger standing to attention on the wing.

On Radio 4 Londoners were being advised to boil their drinking water – 'even if you're only making a cup of tea.' I was glad I was heading north.

That is until I saw the motorway – it was like Oxford Street. If there's one thing more depressing than being in a traffic jam on the M1, then it must be queuing on a slip road for the privilege of joining a traffic jam on the M1.

There was no turning back and I sat in line, inching forward, the Citroën sniffing warily at a Sierra's backside. Four cars further along I could see a would-be hitch-hiker smiling broadly and brandishing a home-made cardboard sign bearing the legend 'Leeds'.

This was going to be embarrassing. It's one thing to fly past at fifty miles an hour, looking straight ahead as though with tunnel vision. But it was going to be difficult to inch past that smile at snail pace – with a bit of luck one of the others would crack before I arrived on the scene.

I specialize in the hitch-hikers other motorists reject and each and every time I do it I tell myself that I will never, ever, do it again. And then it rains and there I am with another drip-dry misfit leaking all over my passenger seat.

I have never picked up anyone who proved to be dangerous, it might be a blessed relief if I did now and then. No – I have an unerring eye for those who have bored for England and are now on their way to take part in the World Championships.

I still hadn't fully recovered from my last encounter. On his back he carried a haversack the size of a small bungalow. It reached down and touched the hem of his corduroy shorts. I should have known, the first rule of the game is never pick up anyone who looks like Frank Spencer. He stuck his beret through the window.

'I'm on my way to Matlock.'

'So am I – jump in.'

77

He eased in rather than jumped in and then sat down with his head between his bare knees, his chin resting on the open flap of the glove compartment. If I had known the sort of conversation we were about to have I would have left it there and probably slammed the lid shut for good measure.

'You can't sit like that.'

His high falsetto voice ran twice around the dashboard before it surfaced up through the hot air vent.

'Don't you worry about me. I'm used to a certain amount of discomfort.'

'Take your haversack off.'

'No, really – I'm fine. Just you carry on.'

The sharp end of a spade nosed its way up through the haversack straps and nibbled at the sun visor.

'Fasten your seat-belt then.'

He tried, God knows he tried, and he only gave up when a loud crack came from his left shoulder.

'Oh dear! I think I've pulled something.'

I opened the boot and he hurled his haversack on top of a sliced loaf, a punnet of strawberries and a packet of fish fingers.

The fish fingers survived, being frozen, but the loaf was a disaster. You can't do anything with a sliced loaf once the slices have gone all triangular, they don't fit in the toaster and poached eggs fall off the end. The strawberries were also a write-off. I could have spread them on my triangular bread.

Still, I was unaware of this at the time and so I slammed the boot shut, settled my hitch-hiker in the passenger seat and set off.

He was an expert on small shrubs and conifers and within a few short miles I knew more about small shrubs and conifers than I ever wished to know.

He also had an overriding compulsion to tell me the name of every tree we passed during the next forty miles.

'Elm,' he would declare as we passed a dying specimen, 'oak – ash – ash – sycamore – willow – willow – lime – oak – another elm, that's two.'

'I can count,' I thought, 'even if I don't know my ash from my willow,' but worse was yet to come. We streaked down a narrow road lined with trees as straight and tall as telegraph poles, one every five yards and he went into overdrive.

'Poplar,' he spluttered, 'poplar – poplar – poplar – poplar – poplar – poplar . . . '

I couldn't take much more of this, he sounded like a cheap Japanese motor cycle, and so I eased my foot down on the accelerator until we were doing a steady seventy miles an hour.

It was nearly the end of him.

'Poplar – poplar – poplar,' his head screwed from side to side until I thought he might take off through the sun-roof, 'polpar – polpar,plopar,plopar,plop, plop,pop,popopopopop . . . '

I had forty-five miles of him and after I had dropped him off in Matlock and discovered my triangular loaf, I thought, 'Never again.' But my nevers last about a fortnight.

The Sierra was now crawling past the young hitch-hiker. It took three stops and starts to beam him from bonnet to boot and now he was grinning in through my windscreen. I nodded and he waved his 'Leeds' sign at me. I leant over and wound down the near-side window.

'I'm only going as far as Huddersfield.'

He jerked open the door.

'Great – so am I.' He slammed the door shut behind him and tossed his sign over on to the back seat. I'd been hooked.

79

'You've got Leeds on your sign.'

'I know – I couldn't find a piece of cardboard long enough for Huddersfield.'

He seemed a pleasant lad. A first-year sociology student and for the next ten minutes or so he regurgitated his teachers' maunderings as though they somehow had a place in everyday life. I leant back and listened – at least he showed no interest in trees, small shrubs or conifers.

I pulled my cigarette lighter and a pack of Dunhill International from my pocket.

'I'd rather you didn't – not while I'm in the car.'

British Rail have made me walk the length of Kings Cross station in search of the smokers' ghetto at the far end of the train. The BBC have banned me from lighting up and the Little Chef tucked me away in a discreet corner, but this was the first time authority had climbed into my own car and asked me not to smoke.

I walked round and opened the door for him, it was the least I could do and he stepped out on to the same square of tarmac he had vacated just a quarter of an hour earlier with a puzzled look on his face as he tried to work out just where he had gone wrong.

The M1 stretched out below me like a freeze-framed conveyor belt carrying the cars of all nations to some great breaker's yard up north. For the past hour or so Minis had performed just as well as Jaguars and the fuel consumption of that white Mercedes had been on a par with that of the miserly Reliant Robin.

He knocked on the window.

'Could I have my sign back, please.'

I reached over and handed it to him.

'Thank you.'

He polished his smile and flexed his thumb and went to work on the Dyno-Rod van behind me. I lit a cigarette and settled down. Huddersfield looked a long way away but at least Aileen was a twenty-Silk-Cut-a-day man.

She had rung me the night before. Sally had answered the phone and feigned surprise that it should be Aileen.

'Hello – how nice to hear from you. Yes, he's here, would you like a word with him?' She covered the mouthpiece with her hand.

'It's Aileen – for you.'

'Well, I never.'

I had wondered just how long it would be before Sally and Nick brought in the heavy artillery.

'Hello, love.'

'Hi! Just thought I'd give you a ring – how are things?'

'Fine.'

'Good. Started writing yet?'

'Just finished a short piece for Ashley.'

'So what now?'

'Don't know yet.'

As conversations go it sort of went and I waited to see how she was going to introduce the television play about Diana into this exchange of fine minds.

'Then what about the two of us getting together on that play about Diana?'

So that was how she was going to do it – very subtle.

'Have you been talking to Sally?'

'What makes you think that?'

Aileen never lied. Never lied, that is, except about her age. She was thirty-nine, she always said, plus VAT, a small service charge and a generous tip. There was no doubt about it though, she had not-lying down to a fine art.

'I thought Sally might have asked you to ring?'

Over in the corner Sally snorted – not a very convincing snort I thought and from the other end of the phone Aileen asked, 'Why would she do that?'

81

'Because she and her sweet little brother are trying to manipulate me into doing something I can't handle yet.'

'I know it won't be easy for you.'

'Too right, it won't.'

'But it could be just what you need – better therapy than writing about cats having their bits and pieces cut off.'

I'd got her.

'How did you know about that?'

'About what?'

'About the cats – having their bits and pieces cut off.'

'It's the sort of thing you always write about.'

'No, it isn't.'

I had no hope of winning this little battle – if I emerged unbloodied from the odd skirmish with Aileen then that was victory enough.

'Now listen, you. Get off your backside and stop moping. Come up here and you can take me out to a literary lunch – I've got two tickets. You can talk to me about cats having their balls cut off and I'll talk to you about what you ought to be doing. Right?'

'Right.'

'Tomorrow then – twelve thirty . . . '

'Tomorrow?'

' . . . and don't be late.'

There was no doubt about it, she had a way with her and a way with me and everybody else. I needed Aileen – she was a healer.

I first met her at a writer's school, it must have been eighteen months previously – Ashley had sent me along.

'Would you like to earn £200?'

'Yes.'

'There are a load of writers spending the week at

Swanwick, a conference or something – I want some interviews.'

'£200?'

'Yes.'

This was remarkably generous of Ashley, there must be a catch in it somewhere. There was – he eventually squeezed thirteen programmes out of my tapes. Compared to Ashley, Scrooge was a pussy cat.

To be honest I wasn't too sure about writers' conferences. I thought they should be at home doing it, rather than sitting around talking about it. Still, £200.

I sharpened my tape recorder and reported for duty. Within the hour I was swept up into the hothouse atmosphere of the place – over three hundred and seventy writers, sweet and sour. All those egos on the loose, looking for a place to perch. The air crackled with love, affection and thinly disguised hatred – I was hooked and I raced around sticking my microphone under an assortment of noses, known and unknown, filling my tapes with the outrageous, the enlightened and the banal.

Julian Symons on crime, Philip Warner on history and Fred Nolan on practically everything else. Ronald Whiting on publishing, Brian Miller on radio-drama and an editor who fell in love with himself all over again as he talked.

I needed a woman's voice for balance and Duncan McIntosh provided it for me – with a little help, of course.

Duncan is a graphologist, one of the best, and a friend of many years. He once read my handwriting on the BBC and told a radio audience that I had a very high sex drive. I have loved him ever since.

'Come with me,' he said, 'and meet Aileen Armitage.'

I fell in love with her the moment her smile burst over me. She was a very attractive woman, her hair the colour of autumn, and those legs, as they crossed and uncrossed, dried my lips.

But when she smiled she was beautiful – she smiled with her whole body. I had no idea that Duncan had such friends.

I sat beside her and tested her for sound. She spoke to me as though no-one else existed – her green eyes boring straight through me.

My first question came out in a high squeaky voice – her answer came back low and languorous. It was bloody hot in here.

After ten minutes my tape ran out but she didn't seem to notice and so I kept her talking for an hour, holding the microphone a few inches below her face and trying not to notice how her shirt front rippled as she laughed. And she laughed a lot, laughed and smiled and never once did she take her eyes off me.

I would have to come back and do this all over again tomorrow with a virgin tape. It's a hard world.

Someone brought us coffee – I didn't know there was anyone else around.

'Thank you,' she smiled and stubbed her cigarette out in the sugar bowl. Duncan had never told me she was blind.

Later that night, at home, I sat on the edge of the bed and waited for the needle to emerge through the back of the canvas. Diana picked her spot on the embroidery and a gentle push sent the merest point to poke its nose out at me. I pulled it through and shifted the angle of the frame slightly so that her hand, encased in plaster and wire, could reach round and take hold of the needle once more. Again she found her mark, this time through the back, and again I completed the move for her.

It was painstaking work. Earlier in the day, when she was at her strongest, she could sometimes manage on her own, but as the day wore on she needed help. It was late now and the pain had taken its toll.

'Go on then – tell me all about it.'

I always found it difficult to get the balance right. I could come home and pour out the adventures of the day, adding a little spice here and there to make it more exciting – regale her with stories that brought the outside world, in living colour, right into her bedroom.

But deep inside me there was a guilt that I could enjoy such things whilst she could only taste them second-hand. Often I felt that my stories only served to highlight the cruel helplessness of her life. And so, often, my stories would begin, 'You haven't missed much . . . ' But of course she did – she missed everything. Tonight however she had seen the light in my eyes and knew that the day had been a special one.

'Well, are you going to tell me or not?'

We put the embroidery away and I played Fred Nolan's tape for her. You didn't interview Fred, you merely pointed the microphone at him and he did the rest. He was wonderful and Diana loved him.

'Who else did you meet?'

She was tiring fast now, her lids were heavy and having their way with her. I massaged her hands and told her about Aileen.

'She was lovely – you'd like her. I'd no idea she was blind.'

I played what little tape I had of our interview as I remade the bed around her.

'She sounds lovely.'

'She is – I think there's another woman in my life now.'

I switched out the light and kissed Diana. She turned over on to her side, willing her limbs to let her sleep.

'Thank God for that,' she said. 'Now I can have the weekends off.'

Chapter 10

The motorway sign read 'Sorry for any delay'. It's a
move in the right direction – a short stab at consid-
eration by an anonymous authority, but after a while
the words take on a depth of sincerity rivalled only
by the taxman's 'your obedient servant' and become
just slightly less annoying than those flashing 'thirty
mile an hour' signs when you haven't moved a yard
in the past thirty minutes.

It had taken a couple of hours to negotiate the twin
hazards of the road works and an articulated lorry now
doing the splits on the hard shoulder. Some beautiful
friendships had been struck in the slow lane, drivers
had exchanged addresses with one another, promising
to write and meet here again next year – I did hear one
or two lurid tales of wife-swopping, but I think they
were somewhat exaggerated.

As the motorway blossomed out into three lanes
once more, the noisy gaggle of cars joyfully skipped
away, one by one, from the coned-off gin trap and
kicked their back legs in excitement as they fought for
control of the fast lane. I slipped the limping Citroën
into the slow lane and spoke to it very firmly – you
have to be cruel to be kind. One note of pity in my
voice and it would be asking for a sick note.

I was already an hour late but Aileen wouldn't have
noticed, she would carry on working until I arrived.
When you are blind you don't look at your watch
all that often.

She stood at the top of the steps, a very small
frown on her face. She wasn't a good frowner,

she had neither the forehead nor the disposition for it.

'You're late,' she declared.

'I'm sorry.'

'We're supposed to be there by now.'

Her make-up was almost immaculate. It was always almost immaculate. She would have sat in front of a mirror staring at a face she couldn't see and worked from memory. The lips were perfect, the eye-shadow faultless. Her eye-liner had been drawn by an artist and the brushwork on her lashes was matched only by the huge blob of mascara that dalmated the tip of her nose.

The little frown tried very hard to be grown up, but it couldn't see the blob of mascara and so the overall effect was about as frightening as that little kitten who growls after the Mary Tyler Moore credits.

'Excuse me.'

I wet my finger and wiped away the black. She waited patiently, eyes shut.

'That it?'

'Yes.'

'Come on then.'

She took me to a large plastic hotel just outside Huddersfield. It looked as though it had been beamed down overnight from outer space, down on to the edge of the moor – lawns and all.

There is a plastic politeness about such places where 'Can I help you?' is a challenge and 'If you'll take a seat, sir, the waitress will see to you in a moment,' is an order.

'Two gins and a tonic, please.'

'That will be £2.75.'

'It's not the happy hour, then.'

'We don't have a happy hour here.'

*　　*　　*

We were ushered into a large dining room and already close on a thousand eyes were dissecting the guests on the top table.

'I read her every Wednesday in the *Daily Mail*.'
'That's not her – this one's Jilly Cooper.'
'Aren't they the same, then?'
'No – this one's got a gap in her teeth.'

I steered Aileen towards the only two empty seats in the room, apologizing on the way to those who had been cracked around the ear by her elbows.

We sat down and friends of hers at the table identified themselves.

'It's Barbara, Aileen.'
'Hello, Aileen – it's Una.'

Aileen turned to the person on her left and winced. 'I wish I hadn't worn this teddy. Don't you find they always pull you up round the crutch?'

'I wouldn't really know,' he told her, in something of a huff.

She hesitated for a split second and then apologized.

'I'm sorry,' she said. 'I didn't realize you were a man,' and that was *his* Literary Lunch ruined.

An operation had restored about 3 per cent vision to her left eye – she could see light and shade but people were just blobs. I had told her that I was an incredibly handsome blob and she had decided to believe me, but usually she worked from deduction and came a cropper a lot of the time.

She was lucky – she didn't appear to be blind at first glance and she liked to keep it that way for as long as possible.

Up on the top table sat Brian Johnstone, an absent smile on his face as he tried to work out exactly where he was today. By his side Alan Plater looked as though he knew exactly where he was and wished he wasn't.

Ringed around the room, as though to stop anyone escaping, were a highly trained team of waiters and waitresses, all with an eye on a woman in a black suit. During the war she would have been SS officer – in peacetime she treated this as a military operation. I turned to Aileen.

'Let's start digging a tunnel while there's still time.'

She didn't laugh because she couldn't see the troops. I repeated the joke to the woman on my right who didn't laugh because it wasn't very funny. The woman in black clapped her hands and the mob moved in on us.

The very rich don't notice waiters. The food simply appears under their nose as if by magic. The rest of us stiffen up and the conversation stops as we sway to our left and stay there at forty-five degrees whilst a bowl of mushroom soup floats through the air. We say 'Thank you' and the waiter doesn't.

All over the room, at table after table, diners slanted their bodies in mid-air and stopped their chatter in mid-sentence.

But not at our table – we didn't have a waitress. Then the swing-doors burst wide open and we did.

She was in her late teens, she was eager and smiling, she was black and broad Yorkshire and she was racing towards us.

'Tha'll have to excuse me,' she gasped, 'I'm not used to all this pressure.'

I would have forgiven her anything – she was smiling and that was enough.

'I'm sorry if soup's cold, but it weren't very warm when they give it to me – I think it's mushroom.'

She told Aileen that she liked her dress and asked her which one was hers.

'Which what?'

'Which fella.'

'This one.'

'I would 'ave guessed him. I like men wi' beards –
me dad's got a beard. Me dad's white – you wouldn't
think so to look at me, would you?'

Aileen had no idea what colour she was. She had
no idea who she was.

'Who was that?'

'That was the waitress.'

'She's nice.'

The woman in the black suit didn't think so and
grabbed the young woman as she pushed her way
back through the swing-doors.

Aileen leant over to me and, as she placed her
hand gently on my thigh, my spine melted. She
always had this effect on me. She was a toucher,
she had to touch, it was her substitute for eye contact
– fingertip vision.

On our second meeting at Swanwick those finger-
tips had traced a delicate path from ear to ear,
taking in my nose and eyebrows as she attempted
to see my face.

'Didn't know you had a beard – I like beards.'

So far so good.

'Laugh lines – that's important.'

I preened.

'Funny nose.'

You could go off people.

'Got a blob on the end.'

Right off.

'Sort of bulbous.'

Can't think what I saw in her in the first place.

'Very sexy mouth.'

I don't know though – she had her good points.

We talked over the mushroom soup. We never had
any problem in finding something to talk about, there
were no awkward silences – it was as though we had
known each other for years.

At first I had felt guilty about my feelings for Aileen. Was it possible to love two women? I loved both Sally and Nick fiercely and equally, but that was different. Or was it?

The waitress was back and clattering the empty plates around the table.

'Have you finished?'

'Yes, thank you.'

'You haven't touched it, neither of you – still, you don't when you're in love, do you?'

She scooped up the two plates and disappeared towards the swing-doors. Aileen took her hand from my knee and we both looked up and grinned stupidly at the others around the table.

I had fallen in love with Diana at first sight and two years later she had fallen in love with me – she fell slower than I did and it took a hundred weekend passes from the Royal Air Force to convince her that this crew-cut erk in the itchy uniform was worth having.

For the next thirty years there had been no-one else and then Aileen walked into my life. I hadn't searched her out – I had so many friends, men and women both, and I loved them all, but none quite like this. This was different.

A silver tray forced itself between us and a black hand rested on Aileen's shoulder.

'Excuse me, love – do you know if I should cut heads off?'

Half a dozen trout waited, mouths open, eyes staring, for the answer as the waitress bent closer to Aileen's ear.

'Only I've never done trout before.'

'I shouldn't bother – just serve them.'

The largest of the fish decided to give her a flying start and fell head first off the sloping dish down on to my plate.

'That's one anyway.'

She went round the table, explaining each time that she'd never done trout before and arrived back at Aileen with the platter bare.

'I'm one short.'

She gave a despairing look towards the kitchen door where the woman in the black suit was on guard duty and then, after a quick plate check, she picked up my knife and fork.

'Here, come on – you've got biggest.'

And she cut it in half and split it between us.

All over the room diners were having quite a nice time, making polite conversation with the stranger on their left and being served with formal precision by robots on their right.

We were having a ball on our table. We were a team now and practised synchronized hysterics as we waited for the next course.

She didn't let us down.

'You'll never guess what,' she shouted from at least ten feet away. 'Black forest bloody gâteau – there's imagination for you.'

She stayed with us during the coffee. A guest had gone to the toilet and so she pulled up his chair and sat down.

'I'm taking catering at Technical College. It's my finals next term – but I shan't pass.'

The speakers did their best but the waitress was a hard act to follow and the afternoon sort of tailed off after she said goodbye.

'Right, I'll go and see if they'll pay me – they don't always, some of 'em go right peculiar on me.'

A thin moorland mist had wrapped itself around the hotel and the Citroën shivered in the car-park – it coughed twice and then died. I was used to these asthmatic attacks and should have parked it on a slope. I hadn't.

'I shall have to give it a push.'

'Shall I steer?'

'I can manage.'

'Go on – let me help.'

'OK – thank you.'

Aileen slipped into the driving seat, nudged off the handbrake and then wound down the window.

'I'm in neutral and the ignition is on.'

'Good.'

I'd just get it out on to the slope and then I'll take over. I put my shoulder to the window frame but the car seemed to have square wheels.

'Am I too heavy?'

'No – we'll do it.'

Suddenly the Citroën took off and leapt across the car-park and I was running alongside trying to keep up. Out of the corner of my eye I could see three pin-striped suits, foreheads down on the boot, their voices echoing what seemed to be the Yorkshire version of a Maori war chant as they pushed.

'No – please!'

'Shove it into second gear, love – wait till I tell you,' one of them shouted.

'She can't.'

We were heading for a line of precisely parked cars and they looked very expensive indeed. Please let us hit a cheap one. I leant in the open window and tried to turn the wheel as I ran alongside.

'How are we doing?' Aileen asked amiably.

'Pull the wheel to the left,' I ordered and she did, so effectively that we now seemed to be going back in the direction from whence we had come. A pin-striped suit flirted off the end of the car and shot off towards Halifax.

'Brake!' I shouted and she did that as well. So well in fact that the wing mirror seemed to pass right through me as I carried on towards Dewsbury.

'Is everything all right?' she asked as I limped back towards the Citroën.

'Tell you in a minute.'

One of the pin-striped suits bent double, steam pumping from his nostrils like a dray-horse. The other was still on the ground, half draped around the bumper.

'Why did she do . . . ?' he panted, looking up from the ground.

'I couldn't get in the car.'

'She was in . . . ' he nodded towards Aileen who had arrived on the scene and was trying to work out where the voices were coming from.

'She couldn't.'

'Why couldn't . . . ?' Very slowly he disentangled himself from the bumper.

'She's blind.'

They looked at one another and then they looked at Aileen who was beaming through the fog. Then they looked at me.

'But, she was driving . . . '

'Well – yes, in a way.'

'I need a drink,' the dray-horse grunted and then he bent to look under the car. 'Where's Brian?'

'He went off that way,' I told him, pointing towards Halifax and they headed off to find him, limping as they went.

'I'm very sorry,' I shouted after them, but my apology just bounced off three broad backs.

'I can drive in theory,' Aileen added and the three paused for a split second and then carried on.

'I can really,' she reassured me and I put my arm around her. If I had one single talent it was the ability to find women with the light of life in them. Diana had that light and now Aileen. I was a very lucky man.

'Come on,' I said. 'Let's try again.'

Chapter 11

I plunged my arm into the washing-up bowl and began fishing about for the chocolate digestive biscuit – if you leave them in hot water for too long they go all horrible.

A few seconds earlier the biscuit had been in my mouth while I juggled with a milk pan in one hand and a mug of hot coffee in the other. Then my mother slapped me on the back and the biscuit shot from between my jaws, skimmed across the sudsy surface, crashed against the Noddy tooth-brush holder she had been de-Macleaning and sank beneath the waves.

'What's that?' she wanted to know.

'It's a McVities chocolate digestive biscuit,' I told her, holding it between forefinger and thumb, the chocolate running down my arm.

'Was it dirty?'

'No.'

'Then why . . . ?'

'Sssh.'

'I beg your pardon?'

'There's a squirrel.'

'Where?'

She bent over and peered into the washing-up bowl.

'Not in there – in the garden, look.'

I pointed out through her kitchen window to where, swinging on a string bag of nuts, usually the property of a blue-tit called Gordon and his common-law wife Elsie, was a young grey squirrel.

My mother dipped her hand into her overall pocket and produced the pair of ancient spectacles Minnie Bonsall had given her.

'Where?'

She wouldn't have been able to see the squirrel if he'd been plucking her eyebrows.

'What's wrong with the bifocals?'

'I only use them when I'm putting my tights on – where is it?'

'He's swinging on Gordon's nuts.'

Fortunately my mother doesn't have a dirty mind and so she took the statement at its face value.

'Gordon will be furious if he ever finds out.'

At that moment Gordon landed on the windowsill and glared at us. Elsie perched on the clothes-line waiting to back him up if things turned nasty.

He was clearly not amused. Sparrows he could deal with, they fell off anyway – without the aid of crampons they were useless – but squirrels were a different kettle of vermin.

My mother tried to explain that he was an uninvited guest and offered to buy some more nuts first thing in the morning. I thought she was being very reasonable but Gordon is the sort of blue-tit who has a chip on his shoulder and tomorrow morning wasn't good enough for him.

Where are the blue-tits who are happy ever after and furtle around whistling a selection from *Snow White and the Seven Dwarfs*? Why do we always get the hard-bitten punks who would kill for a bag of assorted nuts?

Then everything went quiet. Gordon froze in mid-glare, Elsie in mid-pique and the squirrel froze three-quarters of the way through a chomp. For a few seconds, time stood still in the garden and then a bush shivered and Whisky's face appeared, anxious and questioning and framed by green leaves like a soldier on manoeuvres.

It was a strange little face that seemed to have been parted down the middle, black on one side, white on the other and it belonged to a cat who was afraid of blue-tits.

So, why did Gordon and Elsie take off like a couple of Harrier jets when every other day of the week they would have dive-bombed him with a malicious relish? The squirrel held his breath as he tiptoed along the fence and disappeared into thin air – but then he was a new boy and didn't know that Whisky was a congenital coward.

The answer stepped out of the bush and stood shoulder to shoulder alongside Whisky. It had one ear and it had one nostril.

'That's Horace – he's Whisky's new friend.'

Whisky had never had a friend before. His fear of birds meant that he rarely went out into the back garden alone – the three hundredweight bag of assorted nuts hanging from the cherry tree turned the place into a sea of feathers and he didn't like the front garden because he once had a nasty experience with a hedgehog.

So, since very few cats strolled through either the kitchen or the back bedroom where Whisky spent most of his time, his confrontations with fellow felines were few and far between.

'Where did Horace come from?'

'He just walked in through the cat flap and he's been here ever since. Somebody must be missing him.'

He was walking towards us across the garden, content to follow in Whisky's footsteps and as he waddled into sharp focus it was hard to imagine just what sort of person it was who could possibly be missing him.

If Whisky was the Ernest Borgnine of the feline world then Horace was a cross between Boris Karloff and Phyllis Diller. My mother read my mind.

'Looks aren't everything, you know.'

She has a nice line in clichés, but of course she was right. Except that when it comes to cats, a complete lack of fur from chin to chest does tend to tell you something about the owner of that fur.

'I think he's deaf in his left ear.'

'He hasn't got a left ear,' I pointed out.

'He's got a lovely smile.'

It's not often you see a cat that smiles. At a pinch Whisky could manage a sickly grin – it would be unnerving to watch the two of them at it together.

They were now crossing the ironing-board on the rockery and moving towards the lawn.

'Do you think he's a stray? He hadn't a thing with him when he arrived.'

I wondered what she expected him to have with him when he arrived. His toothbrush perhaps, and a spare pair of pyjamas?

'Would you like me to bring the ironing-board in?'

'No – I haven't finished the weeding yet.'

I once wrote to 'Gardeners' Question Time' offering them, free of charge, my mother's topical tip for weeding rockeries. All you need is a trowel, a small fork, a bucket and an ironing-board.

Once a week, after I had cut the lawn, she would tidy up the neat little bed at the end of the garden and then start on the rockery – but this meant standing on the neat little bed at the end of the garden that she had already spruced and so she would fix up the ironing-board at its lowest setting so that it spanned the freshly raked soil and fragile bedding plants like the Clifton Suspension Bridge.

Then, with the bucket in one hand and the fork and trowel in the other, she lowered herself, full length, face down, on to the ironing-board. Slowly the four legs would sink into the soil until the underside of the board brushed the delicate heads of the little plants.

She remained absolutely still until the board had finally settled and then, plonking her bucket down on

98

the rockery and her chin on the asbestos square, she would get cracking with the trowel and the fork.

Every now and then one of the four legs would strike a buried stone and refuse to sink and then the ironing-board would begin to tilt until she flopped off sideways in slow motion down on to the freshly tilled earth. This she accepted as one of the risks you had to take with weeding.

A face appeared through the cat flap – it had one nostril and one ear.

'Good morning, Horace.'

Horace smiled at my mother, nodded politely in my direction and moved over towards a saucer of pilchards by the washing-machine.

I opened the door. 'Come on, Whisky.'

My mother dried her hands on her overall and picked up a second saucer.

'He won't come in just like that. You have to shut the door and make a noise like a pilchard.'

She had me beaten this time, I couldn't ever remember having heard a pilchard – David Attenborough was my constant link with nature but even he drew the line at dolphins.

'Look, let me show you.' She tapped the saucer gently with a teaspoon and within seconds Whisky's furry backside began to ease itself in through the cat flap.

'See?'

'It works, doesn't it?'

'Every time.'

'Can you do a cod in butter sauce?'

We sat at the dining table and I had another cup of coffee whilst my mother worked away at her bottle of Buttercup Syrup and smacked her lips in appreciation. We chatted about this and that. Sometimes it seemed that every time I chatted about this, my mother was

99

chatting about that, but we usually finished together and felt all the better for the experience.

'Have you decided what you are doing about the house?'

I had – almost. But I worried about what the kids might think and what my mother might think. I worried about what the world might think. Aileen had left the decision to me.

'You could move in here,' she had said, *'there's plenty of room and Sally could come with you. Then you can take your time and plan for the future.'*

For me it would be the perfect solution. The house in Matlock wasn't a home any more without Diana and the memories of that final day were waiting for me, cold and clammy, every time I opened the front door.

Both Aileen and her huge Victorian flat with its nine large rooms would give me the space I needed to come to terms with my life. There was a warmth about the house that echoed the laughter of the years – a gentle breath of peace about the place that wordlessly assured no harm would come within these walls. To me it offered both sanctuary and Aileen's calm and tender presence.

But what would I tell the children? 'Well, it's three months now since your mother died – so I'm moving in with another woman.'

Take a deep breath and try it out on my mother.

'I had thought of moving in with Aileen – to give myself time.'

She said nothing – just reached across the dining table and picked up a small bottle of pills. This wasn't fair. There was a generation between us – her own mother had dressed in black for three years after her father died. I doubted if many friends my own age would understand. It wasn't fair on her.

She fiddled with the top on the bottle and it clicked like a time bomb as she twisted it round and round.

'Are you sure about this?'

'Yes.'

'Have you told the children?'

'Not yet.'

She held the bottletop tight in her left hand and screwed the bottle itself with her right, her face a picture of frustration. Was it the bottle or was it me? She gave up, and banging it down on to the table, picked up the Buttercup Syrup once more.

'I can't be doing with that – there's no arrows on it.'

I had spent the best part of an afternoon teaching her how to line up the arrows with one another and now the chemist had given her a press and twist job. I took hold of it.

'It's another child-proof one. You just press and then twist – see how it works?'

She picked it up and had a go.

'How on earth do they expect children to open these?'

'They don't.'

'I should think not.'

She licked her syrupy lips, reached out for the tablespoon and then changed her mind.

'Diana told me all about Aileen.'

'I didn't know that.'

'She liked her – she was a good judge of character.'

'Yes, she was.'

'So, what are you worried about?'

'Sally and Nick, I suppose – and the fact that it's so soon. People won't understand.'

She did a quick press and twist and dropped the bottletop into the waste-paper basket.

'We'll let 'em breathe, shall we?'

She smiled up at me. She'd done just the same with the arrowed top after my hour and a half tutorial.

'You can't go worrying about what people think – you can waste your life doing that.'

101

'It's the kids, really.'

'Try them. They've got a lot of Diana in 'em – they probably read your mind three weeks ago.'

I smiled at her, she could be right. There had never been a generation gap between my mother and the children, or anyone else for that matter. She simply loved and loved simply – she had never doubted the depth of my feelings for Diana and she wasn't doubting them now. She understood and didn't need to ask questions – to have someone trust you like that is a gift beyond price.

'There's just one thing.'

'What's that?'

'You had to do everything for Diana for fifteen years – it was a long time.'

'Yes.'

'Aileen's blind.'

'That's no problem.'

Whisky strolled into the room and dropped his pipe-cleaner on to the hearth. Horace had a sniff at it and then settled down on the rug beside his new friend. Soon they were both snoring, Whisky in stereo – Horace in mono.

'Right then. If you're sure – you go and make her happy. From what Diana said she had a right sod the first time round.'

I had arranged to meet Sally in the Queen's Head for coffee and I was late. She was over in the corner with an empty glass in front of her.

'Sorry, love.'

'It's all right.'

'Another one?'

'Yes, please – Irish.'

Behind the bar Anne was already floating the cream over the black coffee.

'Sally doesn't look very well.'

'No – it's going to take time.'

I walked over to the table and sat down. My daughter had an air of grim self-control about her and her smile was made of glass.

'Are you all right?'

'Yes.'

She seemed to relax and the smile became more liquid as I told her about Horace and about the twist and push bottle. We decided on lunch and she buried her head in the menu. She had a thing about menus – she read them like novels, every word.

Was this the right time to tell her about Aileen and my plans for the move? I was an expert at putting things off.

There was a loud cackle from down by the door as a big blousy blonde got the joke a minute or so after everyone else at her table. Very soon her friends joined in and faces all over the bar began to crease with the infection.

I turned back to Sally and her face was drawn with pain, tears running down her cheeks. She looked at me with eyes that were melting.

'How can they laugh? Don't they know my mother's dead?'

I moved over by her side and put my arm around her shoulder and felt her tears wet upon my neck as her body shook.

'It's all right, darling – you cry.'

She cried and everyone in the bar pretended not to notice and I wondered if there would ever be a right time.

Chapter 12

I leant back and toasted my bottom on the radiator
by the window. The snow had melted and thirty-
five pathetic rose-bushes posed naked like so many
stick insects – a row of go-go dancers that had
gone-gone off.

My garden looked as good as any other garden with
a foot of snow hiding the scars and I never made any
attempt to clear it – I knew what was underneath.

Now it looked disgusting as it simply sprawled
around the edges of the house, unkempt and dissolute.
It was a garden that had given up on life.

I wondered what had happened to the slugs. I had
imagined them, over the winter, entombed in tiny
blocks of ice wondering what the hell had hit them.
I didn't care what the RSPCA thought – I hoped
they had chilblains, frostbite and chapped lips and
it damned well served them right.

Every year we had slugs like the Pied Piper had
mice, thousands of them and they made our lives a
misery.

Sally pushed her way in from the kitchen. She had
a tin of Heinz baby food in one hand and a spoon in
the other. This was her breakfast – we lived well.

'Penny for your thoughts.'

'I was thinking about the slugs.'

She paused, her spoon suspended over the little
tin of apple dessert. 'That's nice – when I'm having
my breakfast.'

I had done battle with the slugs for some twenty-five
years. A corner of the field at the bottom of the

garden was now a large bog where an ancient drain had cracked and seeped over the years. It spawned small frogs and big slugs who were power crazy and determined to take over the world.

Old Mrs Peachey who once lived next door had been appalled by my scientific approach to the problem.

'Have you any idea what those slug pellets do to the poor things?' she shouted at me over the fence. 'They just blow them up until they burst.'

She made me feel like a mass murderer.

'It's so cruel – you want to do what I do and cut them in half with a pair of scissors.'

I didn't feel so bad about it after that. I told Sally about the scissors and she pushed the baby food away from her and poured herself a cup of coffee.

'Never mind, you won't have to bother with them this year.'

'No, I suppose not.'

My bottom was done nicely now and so I joined Sally at the table. We had talked through most of the night and still I hadn't told her about Aileen's suggestion that we move in with her.

'Sally . . .'

The back door shuddered and a whirlwind moved through the kitchen. Empty milk bottles rocked on their heels, the frying-pan trembled and a small bucket screamed in terror.

'I think Nick's here,' Sally said.

He looked very smart in his dark suit and company tie – a far cry from those days of torn jeans and crumpled sweat-shirts.

'Morning.'

He sat down and helped himself to coffee. Now I had both of them together I mustn't put it off any longer. I took a deep breath.

'Where's the milk?' he asked.

'There isn't any,' Sally told him, 'Arthur hasn't been yet – we're using these.' She reached out and passed him one of several thimble-sized cartons she had rescued from a Little Chef. 'They come in very handy – milk or creamer?'

I knew from experience that he couldn't open them without squirting himself in the eye and so I took over the responsibility and squirted it all over his new company tie.

'Sorry.'

'You have to earn these, you know,' he muttered, and then taking in my torn jeans and sweat-shirt he added, '*you* ought to wear a tie.'

'If you remember,' I said, 'you took every one of the ties with you when you got married.'

'They were *my* ties – I *bought* them. You just borrowed them.'

'I got used to borrowing them,' I told him as I sponged his tie with my handkerchief.

'That's my handkerchief.' He took it from me and put it in his pocket. 'Where did you find that?'

'It was all scrunched up into a ball and stuffed between two pipes under the radiator in your bedroom.'

'That's right – that's where I used to keep it.'

'I washed and ironed it.'

'Thank you.'

This was getting completely out of hand. He'd be off again in a minute or so – I took another deep breath and then I noticed his shirt.

'That's my shirt.'

At least he had the grace to look embarrassed.

'Er – yes, it is sort of, but I only wear it when I'm desperate – it has seen better days. Cigarette?'

He offered me his packet. He had just a single Silk Cut left and I took it.

'Thank you.'

He lit it for me and then took a Dunhill International from my packet.

'Have you thought any more about what you are doing? About the house, I mean?'

I took another deep breath – I was feeling quite dizzy with all this deep breathing.

'Only I've been thinking,' he went on. 'Why don't you ask Aileen if you can move in with her for a while – I'm sure she wouldn't mind and you could take time to work things out. The pair of you get on well together.'

I glanced across at Sally and she nodded.

'It's a good idea,' she said, 'why don't you ask her?'

I pulled hard on the Silk Cut – it was like inhaling thin air.

'Well, actually – she has suggested it.'

'Then why didn't you say something?'

What was it my mother had said the other day? *They probably read your mind three weeks ago.*

'I wasn't quite sure how you would take to the idea.'

Sally stood up and put her hand on my shoulder. 'You've got to live your own life, Dad – you don't have to prove anything to us.' She disappeared into the kitchen and Nick stood up.

'Right then – I'll be off.' He finished off the coffee. 'Can I borrow a cigarette, I seem to have run out.'

'Take the packet – I've got another one.' I pushed it towards him.

'No – I'll just have a couple.' He took four and pushed his chair back. 'Sally's right – you do what you want to do and we'll all be happy.' He patted the top of my head and made for the door. 'Bye.'

I always seemed to underestimate the two of them. They had a depth of understanding way beyond their years. I was a very lucky man.

I picked up the cigarette packet and flipped back the lid. It was empty.

*　　*　　*

107

I sold the house just like that. The 'For Sale' board was still quivering as I welcomed the first viewer at the front door.

'This is the kitchen.'

He showed no surprise. Perhaps the cooker, fridge and sink-unit gave the game away. He said very little as he and his wife trooped around the rooms.

'This is the toilet.'

We had left that little room until last as Sally was still sitting on it when he'd rung the bell.

'I need to be in in six weeks – can you be out by then?'

'Yes.'

And that was that. You hear about chains – dozens of houses to be sold as far away as Plymouth and Aberdeen. We didn't even have a link.

The 'Sold' sign went up and we began to gut the place. I cast a weather eye around the dining area. Six chairs, dining table, wall-unit, sideboard, stereo and two thousand books. I could shift that lot in a small van – be in and out in an hour or so.

'I shan't bother with a removal firm, Sally – I'm going to do it myself.'

'OK – you empty the sideboard and I'll start in the kitchen.'

Did you know we had three complete dinner-services? No, neither did I. I thought I could remember seeing the green one with the flowered plates before when Vera came up from Hampshire in January 1969 and I vaguely remembered the rosebud dinner-service because I once broke a cup and heard about nothing else for a fortnight. But I had never set eyes on the white set with the fluted edges before in my life.

I had been in charge of the cooking for twelve years and my cooking doesn't lend itself to posh tables laid out with tureens, white fluted dinner-services and gravy boats. You don't have gravy with fish fingers.

I had stolen a dozen television cartons from behind Charlie Farmer's television emporium on Causeway Lane and two dozen British Sherry boxes from the Winehouse.

Sally was taking the kitchen apart brick by brick, and stacking it all into yet even more cardboard boxes.

'Look – my Peter Rabbit tea-set. I'd forgotten about that.'

'Do you really need it?'

'Yes – I've always loved it.'

'You'd forgotten about it.'

'That's beside the point.'

I unearthed three tea-services and more vases than I have ever grown flowers. The contents of the sideboard alone had accounted for three television cartons and seven of sherry.

'I think I might ring Riber Removals – that sideboard has a false bottom.'

'That,' she said, pointing to three huge packing cases, 'is all out of the small cupboard. Did you know we had thirty-seven egg-cups?'

I rang them next morning and we were still packing a week later when they arrived with the van.

I felt shattered. All through the evening and deep into the night we had a constant stream of visitors who wished us well. Sally kept asking them if they would like a cup of tea and I tried to stop her since we had packed all but two of the cups. I spent most of the evening asking visitor number twenty-two to drink his tea quickly so that I could press the cup into the waiting paw of visitor number twenty-three.

Finally the last loyal friend disappeared into the night and we were left alone in our carpeted desert. I opened the fridge door and finished off the remains of a milk bottle before I went to bed.

Something niggled away in what was left of my brain – something I should have done and hadn't done and at just after half past three in the morning I crawled out of bed and began to defrost the fridge and freezer.

I was wary of the freezer. Once upon a time, as I opened the door, a 3½ lb frozen chicken had leapt out and broken my bare foot. Chickens are incredibly solid little animals when they are frozen, but eventually I had my revenge on him as I pushed the best part of a packet of sage and onion stuffing up his rear end. He was so embarrassed he didn't know where to put himself and so he just lay there on the draining-board and winced.

Che Guevara, the robin, had witnessed this eye for an eye, bum for a foot exercise in reprisal through the kitchen window, and I always felt that the experience had hardened his previously sunny outlook and marked his move into guerrilla warfare.

First I emptied the fridge. There wasn't much in there – just a bottle of orange juice, a garlic sausage, two eggs, two Cornish pasties and a ballet shoe.

Both the fridge and the freezer were the sort that had to be watched as they defrosted and so I spent the remainder of the night jamming bowl after bowl of hot water deep in the lower intestine – then mopping up with kitchen roll and odd bits of clothing that weren't worth the packing.

I had just finished as Sally tumbled downstairs in the morning. I had her breakfast ready for her – a ballet shoe nestling in a fresh bed of lettuce, garnished with a sprig of parsley and a pat of best English butter on the side. It looked quite tasty.

'Where did you find this?'

'It was in the fridge – bottom shelf at the back.'

'That accounts for it then.'

'Accounts for what?'

'The packet of bacon on the top shelf of my wardrobe.'

In the early morning light – without make-up and if I closed one eye, she looked even more like my mother in those early photos. It was very worrying.

I had dreaded the thought of packing up the house. So many memories, so many happy moments to be uprooted and dropped in crate after crate. And yet it hadn't hurt as I had thought it would.

They were already packed inside my head and heart where they would remain for ever. They were a part of me and the house was merely a park where the game had been played.

Only in the bedroom where Diana had spent most of the past fifteen years, surrounded by the things she loved, did the echoes still ring from the walls.

Her clothes were a hurdle that we didn't jump – we had sidled round the edge and, after packing them in a carton, we took them down to a charity shop. That was a bad time – it was as though her whole personality was being folded neatly to be taken away and disposed of.

So much time had been spent in the choosing of them and so much in the wearing that we mentally took a deep breath and held it for half an hour or so while we emptied the wardrobe and tried not to think too much.

I was becoming an expert at putting my brain on hold – with practice one can divorce mind from body and it helps at times.

We kept a couple of things. Sally hung on to the dressing gown that Diana had worn over the last six months, and at night she would pull it around her, snug and warm, feeling close to her mother.

I kept the little red hat that she had bought for Nick's wedding – it had sat by the wreath on the coffin and somehow brought a smile to that final day.

The bathroom I cleared in two minutes flat but the rest of the house seemed to have nothing to do with me – it was as though I had never lived there.

When Riber Removals arrived, my first thought was that they would never get everything in that van – it was far too small. But I hadn't reckoned on it having elastic sides. I still don't know how they crammed it all in – perhaps it had a false bottom like our sideboard.

I acted in an advisory capacity.

'You won't be able to swing the big wardrobe round the corner of the stairs – you'll have to take it to pieces, I had to do that when we moved in – there's a couple of screws . . . '

And then I tailed off as they lifted it high over the banisters and round the corner.

'I'd like to take the stone pig-trough from the garden. You'll need one on each corner, it's very heavy so when you come to move it just give me a shout and . . . '

A movement caught my eye and Mr Shimwell's right-hand man was walking past the kitchen window with the pig-trough on his shoulder.

There's no doubt about it, there's a knack in this removals business and I haven't got it.

Around lunchtime the little van steamed off down the road and made for Huddersfield. It would have been nice to think that after twenty-five years it would have taken at least a couple of pantechnicons to cart all your stuff away, but the little van was very pleasant and seemed to know what it was doing.

Sally and I sat on the carpet and ate the couple of Cornish pasties which we washed down with a half-bottle of wine.

Out on the lawn the birds were demolishing the final contents of the breadbin. It was a civilized rural scene until the starlings arrived and began to duff up

112

the sparrows. Sally would have gone and sorted them out, but her wellies were packed in the van.

In the event she wasn't needed – Che Guevara did it for her. The starlings had very sensibly left him alone up until now, but then a couple of the feathered hooligans rushed him, causing him to drop a small crust of wholemeal sliced.

He went berserk and brought his knee up into a starling's groin. His wing was a deadly weapon and he wielded it like an axe. Within seconds they had gone and, one by one, the other birds returned, giving the little robin a wide berth and the sort of respect we might give to Clint Eastwood.

'Do you think we should tell the new people about him?' Sally asked.

'No,' I told her, 'they'll find out soon enough.'

Chapter 13

A phone was ringing and I couldn't find it on the bedside table. I threw the covers aside, leapt out of bed and ran straight into a fireplace.

Why had I ever imagined that I might now be excused the seven-thirty phone calls from my mother just because I had moved up to Huddersfield?

This was my first morning and I didn't quite know where I was. Where was the phone? Down in Aileen's study, that's where.

I shuffled into my dressing-gown and ran down the stairs – I could tell it was my mother, she rang louder than anyone else. I know it's impossible but she did.

I was surprised that she had managed the intricacies of dialling the new number.

'*You have to dial a code first – it's 0484.*'

'*I shall never manage that.*'

'*Course you will.*'

'*I shall have to practise.*'

'Mum – is that you?'

She'd disappeared. I could hear the Hoover blasting away in the hall. She abused the Hoover dreadfully. Sometimes in the summer, on a nice day, she would carry on through the hall and out on to the drive where she sucked up dead leaves and small lumps of asphalt.

Once, after I had cut the grass with the Flymo, she Hoovered the entire lawn and then came back down the path and did in between the pavers.

Silence, and then the sound of footsteps.

'Hello? Mum?'

'Deric?' The voice was small and uncertain.

'Yes.'

'Thank goodness for that.' The voice was sure of itself again. 'Where have you been?'

'I've been here.'

'Well, I couldn't find you. I've tried everywhere. I had a dummy run with this code thing last night. I talked to a lady just outside Cambridge, she does bed and breakfast and she's very reasonable. She's worried about her son – he's in Belfast in the Army and what with the troubles . . . Anyway, she'd never heard of you.'

'She hadn't?'

'No – I had another go this morning. Where's Sedgewick?'

'The Lake District, I think – I'm not sure.'

'He was a pensioner. He was very nice – he asked me if I ever went down to Stratford-upon-Avon. He does, a lot apparently – you know, Shakespeare and all that.'

'Yes.'

'He's going again in August. He asked me if I was interested.'

'And are you?'

'No. The last time I went I was very disappointed in their Debenhams and they hadn't even got a British Home Stores. It wasn't a patch on Sheffield.'

I suppose once you've seen *A Midsummer Night's Dream* minus the Brussels sprout, you tend to go off Shakespeare.

'Anyway, look – I must get on.'

'Right.'

'What I wanted to know was – how do you fancy a Hostess Trolley that will keep your food piping hot?'

'That's very nice of you, love, but Aileen's got one.'

'Well – what about a stereo stack system?'

'We both have one of those and Sally has her stereo here at the moment – we might blow the roof off if

115

we have another one. Where have you got all this stuff from?'

She ignored me as she often did and had another go.

'What about a superb gas fire with natural coal effect?'

'We're all electric.'

I could sense a touch of frustration creeping in.

'A toasted sandwich maker then – that doesn't seem to be gas.'

'I'm ever so sorry, Mum, but we have one of those, as well.'

I tried to let her down gently and at the same time wondered if she'd thrown a brick through Curry's window.

'Well,' she said sadly, 'it doesn't look as if there's any point in me going in for this competition at all, and you won't want the car – you've got one of them as well.'

'What sort is it?'

She had a look at the form.

'It's a Porsche or something.'

'That would be nice.'

She brightened up immediately.

'Right then – I'll have a go at it. I'll let you know if I win – we won't tell them you've got one already, and Deric . . . '

'Yes, love?'

'Could I come up and have a look at your new house sometime?'

'Of course.'

'And I'd like to meet Aileen, you know – just meet her.'

'I'd love you to. Let me know when and I'll fetch you.'

'We'll do that then, only I don't feel so bad about staying away longer – not now that Whisky's got Horace.'

116

*   *   *

I made myself a cup of tea and sat at Aileen's desk,
looking out over Greenhead Park. It was a wonderful
old flat, my mother would love it. Nine large rooms
sprawled across the top two floors of an Edwardian
mill-owner's house. It had vast leaded windows, each
one capped with a carved wooden pelmet about the
size of a small garden fence.

There was a peace about the place and a maturity
that came only with the years – it was a flat that knew
its own worth and didn't have to prove anything to
anyone any more.

It had helped Aileen heal after twenty-seven years
of disastrous marriage and an acrimonious divorce.
It had wrapped itself around her and welcomed her,
making her feel safe and wanted.

It was her sanctuary and she had been prepared
to share it with no-one. No more relationships, just
the fleeting affair and then back to the warmth and
walnut, to her own place where she could become her
own woman again.

And now she was prepared to share it with me and
already I could feel the magic working.

Just over a year ago Diana had sat over there on the
couch with Aileen. She had needed the rest after
climbing the outside staircase to the second floor,
backwards on her bottom. It was the first time the
two of them had met – they had spoken for hours
on the phone, many more times than they had told
me. Nick let me in on the secret.

'Did you know Mum used to ring the Samaritans?'

'No – I didn't.'

I had felt a sense of failure sweep over me. I thought
that I had coped with everything and now I learnt that
it hadn't been enough.

*'She thought she was ruining your life – she couldn't talk
about it with you, so she rang the Samaritans instead. It*

all started when you had that bit of a breakdown. Then one day she rang Aileen and she never bothered with the Samaritans again.'

Certainly there had been no barriers to break down, no awkward silences as they sat and talked the morning and early afternoon away.

I had left them to it and gone upstairs to saw an inch off the bottom of a bedroom door that wouldn't shut.

'Will he be able to manage all right?'

'Probably not.'

Diana didn't rate me highly as an exponent of do-it-yourself and with very good reason. My reputation in that area was best summed up in a one-liner from my mother-in-law the day she saw a brand-new sink unit waiting its turn on the lawn.

'Is Deric going to do it or are you getting a proper man in?'

It took me an hour to remove six heavily painted screws and then Aileen appeared on the landing wearing a leather jacket and boots.

'We're just going out for a while – Diana's working her way down the steps.'

'I'll come with you.'

'No, you carry on – just get the wheelchair out of the boot for us.'

I stood by the front gate and watched as the woman who couldn't see pushed the woman who couldn't walk to the pavement edge. They waited for a break in the traffic.

'Now!' shouted Diana.

'Right!' Aileen yelled and the wheelchair crashed into the gutter as all four wheels touched the tarmac in their own sweet time – then it pulled itself together, gritted its teeth, and headed straight for the driver's door of a Cortina parked on the other side of the road.

'Hard right.'

'Right.'

Aileen turned hard left and headed for the rear passenger door.

'Stop.'

The driver of a Securicor van did as he was told and pulled to a halt just slightly before Aileen got the message.

'Back up.'

'Right.'

'Now left – that's that way.'

Bob Marley wailed out through the sun roof of a pink Capri as the West Indian driver stood on his brakes.

'Don't worry – we're doing all right.'

'I'm getting the hang of it,' Aileen agreed as she slammed the front wheels into the kerb. Diana shot a foot in the air, hung there for a few seconds, and then tumbled back down on to the waiting cushion.

'Turn it round.'

'Right.'

'Lean it back and pull.'

'Right.'

'That's it – wonderful.'

They moved off – two pilots and an unguided missile weaving an erratic course along the pavement, causing small dogs and large ladies to leap out of their way.

I went back upstairs and tried to concentrate on my joinery. I measured my mark precisely and drew a fine line with my special carpenter's pencil and in no time at all I had shaved exactly one inch off the top end of the door.

They came back as a team. I watched as they crossed the road and this time the instructions were so sophisticated as to be invisible – perhaps Diana was using a whistle that only Aileen could hear.

They examined my handiwork as I opened and shut the door to show them how it now cleared the carpet. Diana watched from a perch halfway up the stairs – all this mountaineering was beginning to wear her out. The adrenalin had lost its fizz and was going flat.

Aileen was impressed as she clicked home the doorknob for the first time in a long time.

'That's lovely.'

Diana was not so impressed.

'What's with that gap at the top?'

'What gap?'

Aileen moved closer and peered up at the door.

'You've got an air-vent, love,' Diana told her, 'you always get a bonus when Deric does a job.'

Now, as I sat at Aileen's desk, I could almost feel Diana here in the room with me. I hoped she would approve of me moving in. I felt she would – or was I just fooling myself?

Come on now. Work – that was the answer. I had Aileen's dining room to turn into an office before lunch.

I had never had an office until Nick married, then I was able to move into his bedroom. Before that I had written for twelve years or so on an ironing-board in the bathroom.

An ironing-board makes a wonderful desk. You have a padded base for a typewriter, at least a couple of reference books can be laid out along its length and the asbestos square at one end provides the perfect landing strip for a mug of hot tea and a cheese sandwich. One of my later models sported two wire shelves underneath that could have been designed especially to take not only an in-tray and an out-tray but also twenty cigarettes, a box of matches and an ashtray.

It had its drawbacks of course. I don't suppose the chairman of ICI has to move all his things to one end of his desk while his half-naked daughter irons her silk blouse on the other and he won't have to put his thought patterns on hold while his son cleans his teeth, combs his tongue and then spits into a sink in the corner.

On the other hand he will never have savoured the pleasure of lowering his desk to bathside height so that he can type with one hand as he soaks away a writer's block.

It's all swings and roundabouts as the saying goes, but now for the first time I had a large empty space and things to put in it.

The old oak table that my father had made was to be my desk. My mother didn't want it any more – it was too big for her new house.

I noticed this fact one day as she came in after feeding the birds in the garden. She re-entered by the French window, fell on her knees, crawled under the table, climbed over the central bar that held the legs in place, then inched her way across the carpet and banged her head as she stood up.

'Why do you have that table across there?'

'Because it's mine.'

It was the sort of argument that always defeated me – her lop-sided logic would turn any further debate into a surrealist session that would make my brain hurt. A week later she told me.

'That table's wrong there.'

'Do you think so?'

'I have to crawl under it every time I come in through the French window.'

And so she gave it to me and it was the most wonderful desk with its solid oak boards and its iron frame and brackets. Chaucer might have sat at such a desk and stared blankly at his Amstrad for hours on end – we had a lot in common.

To cement the bond I christened my new machine by typing in the first line from *The Canterbury Tales*. 'Whan that Aprille with his shoures sote.'

We had more in common than I thought – Chaucer couldn't afford the spell-check software either.

*   *   *

Over the next few days I added bookshelves to my room, carried my filing cabinet in from off the garage roof and stood my trusty Xerox copier on a small coffee table that winced at its coming.

I brought out my portable reel-to-reel tape recorder and sat it by me on the desk. It was the property of BBC Radio Derby and I'd had it on loan for years – they would have forgotten all about it by now.

The scene was set for a period of prodigious output. At last I had the time, whole days of it, whole weeks of it, months of it all to myself. This office was to be the launch pad of a new career – time to start again and I couldn't think of a bloody thing to write about.

The truth was that I was exhausted. After fifteen years of sleeping on the run and eating occasionally I was down to just under 8 stone from 10½ stone and my brain was like a pudding. Every night I had the same nightmare – a woman drowning in a bath. Every night I tried to save her and every night I failed miserably.

I decided to be kind to myself. I had well over a thousand radio pieces on my files – most of them chronicling my domestic life, week by week, over the past fifteen years. They were light pieces that recorded my running battle with role reversal. Maybe the Amstrad and I could edit them down and produce something worthwhile until I could taste my creative juices once more.

In the meantime I kept my hand in with Radio Derby. Every Friday morning I drove down the M1 to the studios in St Helen's Street and engaged myself in a spot of verbal arm-wrestling with Graham Knight, the presenter of the 'Line-Up' programme.

Graham is very quick – he can think on his feet. Fortunately he presented the programme sitting down so I was always in with a chance.

Ashley Franklin produced this extravaganza of words and music with the help of his Filofax and a brand new production assistant. Joanne was slightly smaller than the Filofax, but she had the most wonderful smile that warmed you through to the marrow.

As I watched them directing Graham through the glass it became obvious that there was the scent of romance in the air, and it disturbed me – how could I tell Ashley's wife Francine that her husband was having an affair with a Filofax?

I had revamped a piece that I first broadcast eighteen months earlier – I had changed it beyond all recognition.

'You've done that one before,' muttered Ashley as I slipped back into the ops room, 'twice.'

That bloody Filofax – it knew everything. Joanne smiled at me.

'I liked it.'

'Thank you.'

'So did I the first couple of times,' grumbled Ashley, 'and by the way – the engineers want to see you.'

Many a broadcaster's blood would have run cold at this news. Radio engineers have a knack of dispensing only those snippets of information that are designed to make life unbearable.

I wasn't too worried, I got on well with them – they treated me as though I were almost human and I trotted off towards their lair with a light heart. If they weren't there I could steal fresh tape for my recorder.

It was feeding time, when engineers are at their most dangerous. Ron, the leader of the pack, was out searching for victims but two of his cubs were huddled in the corner, picking over the dead bones of a salad sandwich.

'You not doing football commentaries any more?' asked Kim.

123

'No – I'm giving it a rest for a while.'

'Won't want your tape machine then, will you?' added Jon through a slice of wholemeal multi-grain.

'Well, I thought . . . ' I began.

'Did you – I find that hard to believe,' said Kim as his leader Ron came in through the door, a small news-reporter dangling between his jaws.

'Friday, then,' said Jon, 'You'll have it back here next Friday.'

'Yes – of course.'

'Right then,' muttered Kim.

'Right.'

Ignoring the pleading eyes of the reporter I quickly left the room and didn't look around again until I was reversing the car out of the car-park. It was a good job I got on with them so well.

I drove back through Chesterfield and called in to see my mother. As I locked the car a man carrying one corner of a double-glazed window was striding back up the path.

'There's nobody in,' he told me.

I could have told him that. This man looked quite normal – anyone who had come face to face with my mother for the first time would have been wearing a stunned expression and a matching twitch.

I remembered voting day and the Labour volunteer standing on the doorstep.

'Can we send a car for you, Mrs Longden?'

'That's very nice of you, but I can't today – I've got to go and vote. I'm not doing anything special tomorrow though.'

Quite why she thought he was sending the car I shall never know. Neither did he, but he rallied strongly.

'You're not voting for Mrs Thatcher, are you?'

'No – she's not putting up round here, it's a bloke called Hill.'

He had turned as he reached the gate and looked back at the house as though not believing the exchange had really taken place.

So had the lady from CND a few days earlier.

'Good morning. I'm from CND.'

'Well, there's a coincidence – I'm wearing one of your blouses at this very moment.'

'No, not C & A.'

'It is – look,' and with that my mother bent her knees and swivelled her neck round so that the woman could examine the label.

God had smiled on me when he gave me my mother and I've never trusted Him since.

As always she had left the key in the back-door lock where I could find it. There was no sign of her, but Whisky stood guard by his personal breadbin on the kitchen floor. Usually she left the lid up for him but today it was shut and he couldn't get in. He took a pace nearer the bin and looked up at me expectantly.

I bent down and flipped back the lid and there was Horace fast asleep and snoring at force five.

Here was big trouble. Whisky was a mild-mannered little chap, wary of sparrows and spiders and frightened to death of flock wallpaper and marks on the carpet.

But let anyone, just anyone, lay a finger on either his pipe-cleaner or his breadbin and Whisky became an animal. Horace had been around – he could look after himself, but Whisky had a cause and would be prepared to lay down his life.

He took another pace forward, purred, turned round and shuffled his bottom into the small space beside Horace, then inch by inch eased what was left of his body into the breadbin until his chin was resting on that part of Horace's head where once there had been an ear.

I closed the lid and wondered if he was gay.

There was an empty stillness about the house – a silence with noises off. The morning paper lay flat on the hall carpet. She must have gone out early, it was almost half past one now.

I switched on the kettle and picked up the paper. She never went out early – she enjoyed her first hour of the day watching Breakfast Television over the top of her *Daily Mail*. The paper would have been delivered around seven o'clock.

I raced upstairs and pushed open her bedroom door. She wasn't there and the bed was made. Thank God for that. My heart was thumping as though I had run up ten flights – I felt weak with relief. She could have gone off on a day trip somewhere. I hadn't thought of that.

I was halfway down the stairs when the second wave swept over me. Thursday night was her bath night. Tuesdays, Thursdays and Saturdays were reserved for total submersion and on the other three days it was 'a good stand-up wash'. She had Sundays off.

The bathroom door was shut and I waited outside for a moment or so. Not again, please not again – not after Diana. I took a deep breath, turned the handle and snapped open the door.

Nothing. A pale grey ring around the inside of the bath told me that she had kept to her routine. I must be getting paranoid.

Down in the kitchen I poured a cup of tea, tucked the paper under my arm and walked into the lounge.

She was sitting in her chair by the fire. A cock-eyed breakfast-bowl of cereal sat on her lap and spilled milk over her nightdress.

She saw me and she smiled and milk ran out of the corner of her mouth and dribbled down her chin. She'd had a stroke.

Chapter 14

I knelt down in front of her and tried to remove the dripping bowl from her lap. She gripped it tight with her left hand and shook her head, then she waved the spoon like a flag in front of my face with her right hand.

I let go of the bowl and sat back on my haunches. She stopped waving and held the spoon upright in front of my eyes. Exhibit one.

Her eyebrows arched – did I understand?

'Yes,' I nodded.

She dropped the spoon on to her knee and it bounced off the bowl. The eyebrows questioned me again.

'Yes.' I wasn't so sure this time.

She hung her right arm out to dry in front of her. It was shaking and strangely deformed, out of control and yet dancing in time with her head. Exhibit two.

Then the eyebrows again.

'Right.'

She concentrated very hard and the arm slowed to a shiver. Then she paused, looked at me and went for it.

Slowly she lowered her arm, her hand twisting and turning like a fairground crane until it found the table-spoon on her lap. It made three passes before grabbing and gripping it as you would hold a screwdriver.

She gave a grunt of satisfaction and then launched the spoon towards the bowl. It was some time before she was able to hit the target and I fought the temptation to help her. At the seventh or eighth pass she managed to dredge a slurry of cornflakes and milk and began to head it up towards her waiting mouth.

This was the really hard bit and I held my breath as spots of milk and the odd cornflake made a break for freedom.

She compromised and her head came down to meet the spoon, shaking in the same rhythm as her arm and then success as the spoon disappeared between her lips, to reappear wiped clean.

She gave a big lop-sided grin of triumph and held the spoon aloft as the milk ran out of the corner of her mouth and washed her chin.

'Shtoke – thash wha . . . Shtoke.' She shook her head. 'Shtooppid is wha – bugger.'

I took the spoon and bowl and put my arms around her. Then I fetched a warm cloth and a towel and began to clean her up. It would only take half a bowl of milk to float a canoe.

'Don't worry, love – we'll soon have you right.'

'Shtoke.'

'Only a little one.'

'Bugger.'

Over the next hour or so I learned that 'bugger' is a very handy word when you can only talk out of the corner of your mouth. I heard more 'buggers' than you've had hot dinners before the doctor came and took over.

She hadn't wanted me to call him.

'Na.'

'Yes – I've got to.'

'Na.'

'Yes.'

'Oh . . . bugger.'

He was wonderful with her and she was wonderful with him. She calmed him down and told him not to worry in so many words and gestures and he told her that the first twenty-four hours was a crucial period and she said bugger it.

She decided to treat the stroke with contempt. She took everything the doctor prescribed for her and topped it off with lashings of Buttercup Syrup. Her physiotherapy programme consisted of picking things up and dropping them – more or less what she had always done.

She told the doctor, in one long convoluted sentence, that she had seen many a stroke and this was only a little 'un and you had to get stuck into them straight away.

It took her twenty minutes to say that – in fact the only time her spirit wavered was when I couldn't immediately work out what she was on about. But she kept talking non-stop and I nodded and pretended to understand every word.

When the doctor returned at tea-time, to check up on her, she met him by the dustbins with the dustbin lid hooked over one hand and an empty cat-litter tray in the other. I hovered within catching distance and hoped he understood.

'You'll be staying tonight?'

I told him I would and he left me to it until morning. When a neighbour called round for a few moments, I nipped out to buy a toothbrush and as I returned I could hear the Hoover blasting away in the lounge. I walked in to tell the neighbour not to bother and found that she wasn't. She was sitting on the settee while my mother combed the carpet for cornflakes.

She tired rapidly after that and I tucked her up in bed and sat with her while she continued to practise her oral physiotherapy. You had to keep talking was the gist of her message, but as she grew even wearier it became difficult to make out one word in a dozen.

She slept and I didn't. I couldn't bear the thought of losing another so close and yet so far, and so

129

I shifted between the two rooms a hundred times during the night.

It would be so cruel if she lost the gift of speech. It was a gift she treasured – I had known her travel eight miles past her bus stop because the conversation with a total stranger had reached an interesting point.

As the night wore on I roamed around the house making endless cups of tea and reporting back on the state of play to Whisky and Horace.

There had been a tremendous racket downstairs just after midnight – it sounded as though an enamel bucket had gone berserk and as I opened the kitchen door there was this mobile breadbin limping across the lino tiles towards me.

I rolled back the lid and two small cats, each suffering from terminal cramp, staggered out and collapsed in exaggerated agony as though hoping to be awarded either a penalty or a saucer of Whiskas Supermeat with Salmon and Tuna.

Horace, believing that visiting was limited to two people per patient, popped out for an early morning vole-crippling session in the garden next door. Whisky, who was frightened of voles, sat by my side on the bed and kept an eye on my mother.

She slept well enough and we kept our fingers and paws crossed in the hope that, when she awoke in the morning, her first words would come out smooth and freshly laundered.

I loved the way she had with words. Some people have a flair for arranging flowers – my mother arranged words, perfectly ordinary words, and the result was a display of shape and colour that was hers alone.

I remembered her standing by the kitchen window, looking out as the clouds burst. She came over and sat with me at the table.

'You know, Deric – ten minutes of this rain will do more good in half an hour than a fortnight of ordinary rain would do in a month.'

I also remembered the phone call one Saturday morning when she told me the latest news about the neighbours.

'They've got a new dog.'

'What sort of dog?'

'It's an ex-greyhound.'

I had wondered what sort of dog it was now – a dachshund, perhaps? I knew what she meant really, but there were other times when I never quite managed to unravel her words.

'I went to town the other day and I was so ashamed – I was wearing odd tights.'

How can you wear odd tights? It's kept me awake at night for the last twenty-five years.

Now and again there were flashes of sheer genius.

'Was your mother left-handed?' I once asked her.

'Do you mean left-handed as she was or left-handed as you looked at her?'

I thought about that one for a moment or so.

'Left-handed as she was.'

'No – but I've got a photo where she is. It's the one where your Aunty May is standing on a chicken.'

I've spent hours looking for that photo.

My father never shared my delight in the way she juggled with words or the way in which she lived her life.

She believed in God and yet never went to church. She took in four spinster sisters, one after the other, and nursed them for years until they died. Jessie, who my mother thought was a thoroughly selfish old woman and a pain in the arse, was with her for seven years – seven hard years during which my mother watched television programmes on euthanasia with a mounting enthusiasm.

But she never seriously considered that she had any other choice but to take care of her – just as it was Jessie's God-given right to be obnoxious.

She believed in the freedom of the individual.

'I don't want to go to school today, Mum.'

'Well, don't then.'

It's no way to bring up a kid and maybe my father had a point, but on the other hand the days I spent with my mother taught me a lot about love and about life and people.

She never judged anyone. Once she saw a punk standing at the bus-stop near her house. It was in the early years when punks were brand-new and frightening. This one was all in black – his shredded jeans and studded leather jacket, his skin and his finger-nails. Only the safety-pin through his nose punctuated the deathly image – that and his bright green hair.

The neighbours shuddered as my mother raced up the path and shouted through the pouring rain.

'You can't stand out in this – your hair'll run.'

She hustled him into her lounge and pointed out through a rear window.

'Keep your eyes open and you'll see the bus coming a quarter of a mile away – you'll have plenty of time to get back out.'

She gave him a cup of tea and a slice of Bakewell tart and they discussed his safety-pin, of which she seemed to approve, and his earring, which she thought was gilding the lily a bit.

Then another punk trundled up to the bus-stop, his purple hair glistening with raindrops.

'That's my mate,' muttered the humanoid through his Bakewell tart. My mother took one look and told him.

'I'm sorry – but I couldn't have anyone with purple hair in my house.'

It was as though she had a ley-line running under her brain that caused her to think at right angles. Whatever it was – a little piece of that brain had gone walkabout and all Whisky and I could do was to sit tight and wait until the morning to see if it came back home.

She was still asleep when the doctor arrived on his way to the surgery. He followed me upstairs and into her room and we stood by the bed and watched her for a while.

At rest her face seemed quite normal. Then she opened one eye, saw us and smiled and it went all skew-whiff. Her right eye butted up to the side of her nose and her mouth slipped off the end of her chin. My heart dropped and nudged up to my navel.

'Good morning, Mrs Longden,' said the doctor.

'Good morning,' said my mother, 'what time is it?'

'It's just after a quarter past eight.'

'My God – you must think I'm ill.'

Every word came through as clear as a bell and even the cat couldn't help smiling.

Over the next hour or so her face moved back from Hyde to Jekyll and although, now and then, she still had to chew her words a few times over it seemed that things were going well. The doctor had been very pleased and not a little surprised.

'She knows what she's doing, so give her her head – just make sure she rests when she's tired.'

He also gave a warning.

'Quite often they have a second one – so keep an eye on her.'

She had slowed down both mentally and physically. In fact at times she seemed quite bewildered by what was going on around her.

'Where do I keep the cat food?'

'In there – here, I'll do it.'

'No – let me. It's good for my hand – exercise.'

133

She took the tin opener out of the drawer and after quite a fight she had the lid off and two saucers filled with tuna Whiskas.

She was well pleased with her little triumph and then she frowned.

'What's this?'

'It's a tin opener.'

'Whose is it?'

'It's yours.'

'Is it?'

'Yes.'

She examined it closely and then shrugged.

'Ah well.'

And then she opened another tin and filled two more saucers, this time with pilchard Whiskas. Horace and Whisky never said a word.

I stayed for a couple more days while she grew stronger and became her old self again. She had always been a past master at 'putting her feet up for five minutes' and now she had it down to a fine art.

She worked hard at her self-imposed physiotherapy programme, which included washing both cats in the sink at the same time, an exercise that should be studied by hospital professionals the world over; and to this performance she added a selection of songs from the shows, beginning with *Lilac Time* and moving through to *The Boy Friend*. This was designed to firm up her speech patterns and had the built-in advantage of stunning both cats into total submission.

But most of the time she was 'putting her feet up for five minutes'. Sometimes she would 'put her feet up for five minutes' twelve times in an hour.

'Make sure she has plenty of rest and some exercise.'

I reckoned I was doing a good job.

It had been four days now and although I had nipped out and bought two sets of clean underwear, a shirt and two pairs of socks, together with a tube of decent toothpaste and a deodorant, I longed to have my own things around me.

I was sure she would be all right if I called every other day and the neighbours had volunteered to set up a spy network and let me know her every move.

She anticipated me.

'I shall be all right now if you want to go home – I can always phone you.'

I detected a note of reluctance – she didn't want to be left on her own again.

'I can stay a couple more days if you want.'

'No – please, I can't bear being watched all the time. You go, I'll be all right – I've got Whisky and Horace. Shall I get your coat? Where is it?'

Of course I could have been wrong.

There were just one or two things I had to do before I left. My mother was in the kitchen perking up Whisky's quiff with a comb. I'd used that comb this morning.

'I'm just going along to the chemist for your tablets – is there anything else you want?'

She thought for a moment.

'I could do with half a cucumber.'

'I'll see if they'll put it on your prescription. Is that it? Half a cucumber – nothing to go with it?'

She had another think.

'A couple of HP11 batteries.'

What on earth was she going to do with this cucumber? Perhaps it was best if I didn't ask.

I was pushing open the garden gate when she unclipped the lounge window and shouted.

'If they've got any rubber gloves bring me one.'

'OK.'

The car was fast asleep at the top of the drive. Better not disturb it – I could walk. I set off and then stopped. She was still hanging out of the window. I turned towards her.

'Bring you *one*?'

'Yes – right hand.'

And then she swung round with her back to the window, thought for a moment and yelled, 'no – *left*.'

It was a cosy little shop. You had to ask for everything unless you had an hour or so to spare. Fortunately I didn't have to ask for half a cucumber.

Outside the hairdresser's window next door was a seed box, raised on a couple of bricks, and it contained several half cucumbers and a selection of home-grown tomatoes.

A young girl had gift-wrapped it for me in red paper as though I intended it for a present and it smelled vaguely of Elnett. I was just glad that I hadn't had to ask for half a tomato.

The chemist was stock-checking contraceptives as I approached the counter. He had a smile for everyone and gave me mine.

'Two HP11 batteries, please.'

'There you are.'

It was a small shop and he hardly had to move for anything.

'You wouldn't happen to have such a thing as a left-hand rubber glove, would you?'

I braced myself – waiting for him to throw the batteries at me.

He beamed and immediately stopped dusting the little packets.

'You're not Mrs Longden's young lad, are you?'

It must have been over thirty-five years since anyone had called me Mrs Longden's young lad, but I admitted it.

He bent down and from under the counter produced a polythene bag containing a single rubber glove – bright yellow, left hand.

'There you are.'

I was really quite touched and I began to thank him.

'It's very good of you – I know she sometimes seems to be a little . . . '

He stopped me.

'Not at all. It began about five years ago when one of my gloves had perished in the bag – your mother bought the other one for half price because she thought it would help me out, and then she bought one out of another packet and it's been going on ever since. She's always one glove behind, but she never lets me down.'

I paid him and he went back to his dusting.

'Thanks, anyway.'

'Not at all – she's a lovely woman.'

He was right, she was.

Chapter 15

Aileen hated the winter months. For several years she was without sight and then an operation had restored a little vision to one eye – about three per cent.

As long as there was sunshine she could see light and shade and people were large blobs, but in the miserly gloom of winter she was back to square one again.

I learnt the basic rules very quickly – much faster than the average guide-dog.

'Small step – couple of strides.'

She nodded and her tongue licked her lips as she concentrated.

'Now.'

She lifted her foot to small step height and then plonked it down in mid-air. Her body pitched forward and I caught her by the scruff of the neck as she dived full length towards the pavement.

'You're supposed to tell me whether it goes up or down.'

Eventually we developed a technique by which I was able to warn and steer her just by squeezing her hand. It worked very well – sometimes too well.

As we ran back laughing towards the car in King Street a traffic warden moved out of the shadows and leant on the bonnet.

'You see this,' he said, pointing at the orange badge on the windscreen. 'This is to allow disabled people the freedom to park wherever is convenient for them to do so if they so wish to do so and feel necessary at that particular moment in time. Now I watched the pair of you walk away and I've watched the pair of you run back and there isn't a bloody thing wrong with either of you.'

We couldn't stop him – he went on.

'I think it's most despicable to deprive a disabled driver of this particular space and worse than that, when the public sees what's going on they lose all patience with the genuine cases. Moreover it's an offence under . . . '

We couldn't get a word in – I felt sorry for him. Eventually he ran out of steam and glared at us in silence.

'Is it all right,' Aileen asked him gently, 'if I'm blind?'

He took a pace forward and peered closely into her clear green eyes. You couldn't tell. He turned to me.

'Is she?'

'Yes.'

'Oh, shit.'

He turned and walked away up the street past the travel shop.

'Oh, shit.'

He reached Burtons and disappeared from sight and then, after a few seconds delay, round the corner, all on its own came a faint and final apology.

'Oh, shit.'

There were also indoor rules. Cupboard doors had to be shut or they nearly took her head off. Her things had to be left where she had put them if she was ever to find them again and she was to be kept away from the cooker at all costs.

I once watched her make a mug of tea. She hung a finger over the rim of the mug and poured the boiling water from the kettle. She poured until the rising water hit her finger and then she yelped, yanked it out and stopped pouring.

'Would you like one?' she asked.

'No, thank you,' I told her.

I didn't want to go through the agony of watching that again and from that day on I made the tea and did all the cooking and there were shouts of great rejoicing down at the Huddersfield branch of Marks & Spencer. I was no great shakes with a cookery book but I could understand every word written on the side of their boxes.

We ate out a lot to vary the menu. Splendid as it is you can get sick of Chicken Kiev with Mushroom and Vegetable Bake, and what's more you begin to feel at home in a new town when the waitress in Pizzaland recognizes you straight away.

'I know you – you're the small Passionara with no olives, aren't you?'

To almost everyone else in Huddersfield I was Mr Armitage. The phone would ring.

'Mr Armitage?'

'Er, no – not exactly, I'm her . . . '

What was I? It became very complicated. Boyfriend sounded rather juvenile. Lover was a little too exotic for Huddersfield.

'She's my mistress,' I tried on one occasion, my tongue firmly in my cheek, but the caller couldn't see my tongue and put the phone down on me.

Aileen's mother wasn't entirely happy with the arrangement. She worried what people might think of her famous daughter.

'This woman stopped me in the Town Hall yesterday and she said she'd been talking to my common-law son-in-law.'

'What did you say?'

'I told her you weren't – I said you were her manager.'

So I became Mr Armitage – it was easier.

* * *

My mother was doing well. I had driven down to see her every other day for the past two weeks. Nick called in on the days I missed and the neighbours seemed to borrow a cup of sugar every hour on the hour judging by the frequency of their telephone reports.

'She's hanging out some washing.'

'Thank you.'

'Thought you would want to know.'

She had never had so much company in her life. Sally was staying with her over the weekend and doing a few odd jobs – she rang for help.

'Do you know where she keeps her screwdriver? Every time I ask her she says she's got my grandad's giblets in the shed – I daren't look.'

'I think she means gimlet – all his old tools are in there.'

'Well, that's a relief.'

'What needs doing?'

'She's unscrewed all the doorhandles.'

'Why?'

'She doesn't know.'

That worried me. *She* usually knew what she was doing even if nobody else did.

Sally had given notice to the casino in London and moved back to the Metropole in Manchester. There she was only a short train ride away from Huddersfield and back amongst her old friends.

She shared a flat in Cheetham Hill with Cathy and Jed. She and Cathy shared a single room, a double bed and many sleepless nights and days. She also had the dubious honour of now holding a one hundredth share in an extremely battered old dog along with Cathy and Jed and ninety-seven incredibly tough little fleas – they had to be tough to survive the arctic temperature in the flat.

Sally was on the look-out for her own place and Cathy, who had sacrificed not only her privacy but

141

also her God-given right to have a good stretch and a cough, wished her well. The fleas would miss her terribly.

Croupiers work strange hours and eat breakfast before going to bed, and in London Sally had worked at nights and spent her days sleeping at Lord's during the boring bits in the cricket.

Now, whenever she managed a couple of days away from the casino, she hurried over to Huddersfield where she would immediately fall unconscious for twenty-four hours and then toast herself in front of the fire until she was done. It was just like the old days – almost.

She had approved of Aileen at first sight and Aileen had welcomed her with open arms. They talked together and they laughed together – but they talked too much and they laughed too loudly as though this was a stage play and they were acting out the parts they were supposed to play.

The daughter – still grieving over her mother's death, but prepared to accept the new woman in her father's life because she knew she was good for him.

The woman – realizing that she must not take over the mother's role, trying desperately to be the older friend and confidante.

I watched their goodbyes as I waited to take Sally down to the station. They wrapped their arms around each other, their cheeks touching and they said all the right things.

But I could see Sally's face as she rested her chin on Aileen's shoulder and it had that brittle touch of glass about it – this will make Dad happy.

Then Aileen's face, the smile so bright it was infinitely sad – this is what Deric would want.

They were both trying so hard that they couldn't be themselves with one another. They were touching and yet the distance between them was vast. It was all too soon for Sally and, because of that, impossible for Aileen. I should have waited – I should have known.

There was never going to be another woman after Diana. This was something I had known and never questioned. For the last fifteen years of her life, every day had been filled with a crippling pain and the gnawing frustration of not knowing why.

And I had watched her take it all and rise above it until pain was just something you had – it was normal. Now let's get on with something important.

So what chance would a new woman have, no matter how much I loved her? What if she complained because she had a cold? I would be forever comparing her with Diana and that wouldn't be fair – you had a right to complain when you had a cold. I did.

Then into my life walked Aileen. A woman who treated her lack of sight as some minor inconvenience and felt it wasn't even worth the mentioning until she stubbed her cigarette out in the sugar bowl.

She was easy to love. It was a new experience for her – to be loved without reservation, to be given the freedom to be herself.

We had been to a party and had a whale of a time. She had laughed with the ladies and flirted with the men – she couldn't help flirting, it was just something she did and since she assumed that all the men she couldn't see were handsome and debonaire she brought a lot of joy to those who hadn't been chatted up in years.

Aileen broke the contented silence in the car on the way back home.

'Good party, wasn't it?'

I smiled in the darkness.

'I've never been so ashamed in my life.'

143

It was as though I had hit her. Her face broke into pieces and her body went stiff and then she cried.

Throughout the twenty-seven years of her marriage she had been told never to tell anybody anything – they might use it against you, always be on your guard. At parties he had sat in a corner and kept himself to himself and if she hadn't, then on the way home there would be an ominous silence.

'What's wrong?'

'If you don't know, I'm not telling you.'

Yet another long silence.

'I've never been so ashamed in my life.'

Then all hell would be let loose followed by weeks of brooding recrimination. And now it was happening all over again.

It took no time at all to prove that it wasn't, that I had meant it as a joke, but I learnt in the process just how thin was the veneer of self-confidence and how tender was the scar tissue that covered the wound.

Sally found a flat in Latchmere Road and I drove over to Manchester to help her move her things. She seemed to have cornered the market in bean bags and so it took several trips.

The flat was small and cosy. Compact was the way Sally had described it on the phone and that was about it. The tiny first-floor sitting room had a window overlooking a pigeon and the kitchenette was just about the ette-est I had ever seen. The bedroom was slightly bigger than both rooms put together and she only had to share a bathroom which was a much lesser evil than sharing a bed. It was cheap and small enough to be heated by heavy breathing, but above all – it was hers.

'Shall we have a cup of tea?'

'Lovely.'

I cleared a bean bag off the settee and sat down. Sally backed out of the kitchenette with a mug in each hand, moved a bean bag off a bean bag and sank into the biggest.

'Cosy, isn't it?'

'Very.'

'Doesn't the television look huge in here?'

I couldn't see it – there was a bean bag in the way.

'Dad?'

'Yes.'

'I do like Aileen, you know.'

'I'm glad.'

'She's perfect for you – it's just . . . '

'Just what?'

'I'm like that with everybody, you don't see me with my friends. It's not just Aileen – even with Jane I feel distant, as though I'm standing over on the other side of the room watching myself talk to her. I can't describe it.'

She had described it very well. I could remember that feeling when Diana had been dreadfully ill and the stress had been at its height. Me watching myself and criticizing my every move.

'Promise me something.'

'Yes.'

'Ring me every day. And talk to me – don't act, don't just tell me what you think I want to hear. Tell me how you feel, every little thing.'

'OK.'

'And tell Jane how you feel. She'll understand.'

Nothing in life really teaches you how to deal with these things. You muddle through and hope that it's enough. Sally came over and sat with me on the settee, her head on my shoulder, and for an hour or so we talked out loud a mishmash of thoughts that sprang from love and fear.

A psychiatrist overhearing us might have permitted himself a wry smile, but I doubt he could have done any better.

It was getting dark outside and Sally had to be at the casino in half an hour.

'I'll drop you off on the way home.'

'Thanks. By the way I've got a present for you.'

And she gave me three bean bags to take home with me.

There was a note from Aileen waiting for me on my desk when I arrived home. Her notes were instantly recognizable – six words, each letter an inch and a half high, scribbled on a sheet of A4. I stepped back a couple of yards so I could take it all in.

'Gone over to Bridie's – back soon.'

The 'back soon' had dribbled off the sheet of A4 and spread across the right-hand page of an accounts book I had left open on the desk.

Bridie O'Connell would have poured a couple of shots of Jameson's Irish whiskey by this time, large ones so they wouldn't have to keep going back to the bottle and they would have settled down for the duration. I sat at my desk and began cleaning up my accounts book and then the phone rang.

'Mr Armitage?'

'Yes.'

'It's B&A Electronics here – I've got some bad news for you, I'm afraid.'

'What's that?'

'The stereo I picked up this morning. We've had it to pieces and it's a write-off – can't do a thing with it.'

Aileen had thought it might be on its last legs – good job we still had mine.

'Well, never mind.'

'The thing is, there's a £10 calling-out charge and we've spent another hour on it already.'

'I see.'

'What we could do is – if we scrap it and I use it for parts, we can call it quits.'

'That seems fair enough.'

'Right then.'
'Right.'

Aileen sailed back home just after midnight. A couple
of Bridie's Irish nightcaps did nothing for her eyesight,
but they boosted her confidence sky high.

'A man rang about your stereo. It's a write-off,
I'm afraid.'

'Oh, dear.'

'I told him to scrap it – it was very old.'

'Seems a shame.'

'Would have cost £20 or so otherwise.'

'When's he coming for it?'

The significance of this last remark took a full half
minute to sink in. I walked slowly over to her study
and opened the door. There was the stereo unit
fast asleep by the fireplace, warm and cosy in the
flickering light.

'Ring and tell them,' suggested Aileen after I
confessed.

'I can't remember the name of the firm. It could
have been anything. B&Q or V&D – anything.'

I spent the next half an hour combing through the
phone book but came across nothing that rang a bell. I
can never understand this desire to reduce everything
to initials. Where would Fortnum and Mason be if they
had called themselves F&M Grocers?

Somewhere in Huddersfield there was a Mr Armitage
who would shortly discover that he had agreed to have
his stereo scrapped and he would never know who had
given that order. Until now, of course.

The phone rang once more. It was almost a quarter
to one in the morning.

'That'll be the shop.'

'Not at this time.'

I picked it up. It was my mother.

'Deric?'

147

'Yes, love – what's wrong?'

'Nothing.'

'Are you sure?'

'Yes – I just wanted to tell you that it's Mother's Day on Sunday and you're not to go buying me anything. Do you hear?'

'Yes, love.'

'It's nothing but a racket and you mustn't go wasting your money.'

'Just a few flowers.'

'No – I don't even want a card. I've been talking to Minnie and we've agreed.'

'All right then – if that's what you want.'

'It is. Anyway look – it's getting late, I'm just going to walk Minnie home, it's dangerous at night.'

'What about you?'

'I shall have Minnie with me.'

'Yes, but what about on the way . . . ?'

She had rung off.

Chapter 16

Every year, ever since I left home, my mother had rung me on the Friday before Mothering Sunday to tell me not to buy her anything.

The timing was crucial. I now knew that the big day was the day after tomorrow and I still had the whole of Saturday to buy her a card and a bunch of flowers.

Only once during all those years did I take her at her word and I shall never forget the look on her face – it was as though I had hit her with a cricket bat.

Aileen thought it was a good idea.

'It is a racket – I told my kids not to buy me anything years ago and they never do. It's a waste of money and they can't afford it.'

'Yes – but she doesn't mean it.'

'Neither did I.'

We had already agreed that I should go and spend the weekend with her in Chesterfield. I wanted to see how she coped over a couple of days – I worried about her unscrewing all the doorhandles, it seemed a strange thing to do.

I parked in the town centre and walked towards the parish church. Under the shadow of its crooked spire stood the little shop Diana had opened some twenty years before.

She had called it 'Slipstream' and she had been so nervous at the thought of her first business venture, but she stuck to it and in no time the little shop was thriving.

It was tiny but it had been a good place to learn and make mistakes before she opened a much larger one in Matlock Bath. Then the paralysis had crept over her and that was that.

It sold children's wear now and I didn't want to look up at the new name and so I walked away and went in search of a card shop. I had been wise in moving to Huddersfield to a new life and a fresh start – here there were memories hiding behind every corner, waiting to pounce.

I walked into a shop on Knifesmith Gate and the first person I saw in there was my mother. She was browsing through the Mother's Day cards and reading the verses. When she found one she thought appropriate she would read it aloud to the person next to her. She was surprised to see me.

'I told you not to bother.'

'I wouldn't dream of not buying you a card.'

'That's nice of you. Look – since I'm here, why don't I choose one?'

I told her I thought that was a very good idea and for the next twenty minutes she closely examined almost every card in the shop, laughing uproariously at the funny ones and shedding a silent tear at the more poignant verses.

To kill time I moved through the various sections and seemed to have covered everything from Happy Birthday to Congratulations on your Vasectomy by the time she came over with a card in her hand.

'I can't make up my mind between this one here and that one in the box up there.'

That one in the box up there was priced at £9.75 and I suggested that perhaps three-feet-square cards in boxes were just a little bit vulgar.

'Do you think so?'

'It's for a wedding anniversary.'

'It's nice though, isn't it?'

150

She settled for the one in her hand.

'You're sure?'

'Yes.'

'Right.'

She gave it to me and I passed it over to an assistant who found the appropriate envelope and put it in a bag.

I handed over a £1 coin, took the 1p change and gave the card to my mother. She was horrified.

'No – it's not until tomorrow. You mustn't give it to me now or it'll spoil the surprise.'

'I'm sorry, love.'

'Besides, you've got to write in it.'

We went our separate ways. Me to buy flowers and she to have a cup of tea and a wholemeal scone in the Town Café with Minnie Bonsall and Nellie Elliot.

For some reason I wanted to go and have a look at my old house in Matlock. I must have passed the end of the road a dozen times since I had sold it, but each time I had put my foot down and sailed on by. Now I felt the need to see it again – the house where Diana drowned. To get it out of my system.

A quarter of an hour later I turned the car into Gritstone Road and on into Bentley Close. Little had changed. There was Chris making love to his car with a chamois leather and across the road Doreen Gascoigne sat in her window and pointed Cliff in the directions of the weeds.

The house looked empty. I opened the car door and walked to the top of the drive and there, leaning against the fence, was my sink unit.

I was furious. What the hell was wrong with my sink unit – it was a perfectly good sink unit, it had years in it yet.

Then I saw the kitchen cupboard. What the hell was wrong with my kitchen cupboard – the effort we had spent in keeping it alive. It must have had thirty coats of gloss paint since we first brought it home as a pup, the doors were twice as thick now – they were like glass.

I couldn't take any more of this. I jumped in the car and drove off down Steep Turnpike into Matlock – if I'd known they were going to vandalize the place I would never have sold it to them.

The football ground loomed up on my left looking lonely and dejected as though someone had ripped out all its sink units. The Town must be playing away today – I wondered if it understood why nobody bothered with it every other Saturday.

I parked the car and tried the main gates – they were locked. Down the road there was a gap in the hedge. I remembered that gap.

One Tuesday evening, a larger than average crowd – there must have been almost five hundred in there and I was commentating for Radio Derby when we saw a small boy, eleven or twelve years old, squeezing his way through the gap in the hedge.

'Fred,' George Bonsall shouted. 'There's a lad down there. coming in through the hedge.'

Fred Shaw eased himself out of his seat and sighed. This wasn't what he was here for. His job, as a lifelong fan, was to play hell with the Matlock players and shout abuse at the referee – he hoped someone would take over in his absence.

He hurried as fast as his legs could carry him, a gentle trot in other words, and we watched as he approached the hedge.

The lad was stuck and Fred, thankful for the chance to keep his hand in, hurled abuse at him instead. After a long and painful struggle the little boy fought his way through the undergrowth and fell, scratched and bloodied down on to the grass.

The football had moved into an aimless phase as the home team struggled without Fred's constant advice and so I concentrated the commentary on the battle down at the hedge.

The lad was standing now, wiping the mud from his trousers and explaining himself with eloquent gestures to Fred who, for once, was listening attentively.

They shook hands and parted, the boy taking up a position behind the goal and Fred wandering back to his seat under our window.

'What was all that about?' George wanted to know.

'It's all right,' Fred turned and assured him. *'He showed me his card – he's a scout for Sheffield Wednesday.'*

As I leant on the gates one of them creaked and inched open. I went in and stood on the terrace. It was a nice little ground – it reflected the people who ran the club. Cliff Britland, the chairman, who never seemed to watch a single minute of a match – he disappeared for long intervals and then reappeared to ask the score.

Sam Fay, the *Mercury* reporter, who had been here almost as long as the stand and knew everyone and everything. He loved the team as though he had given birth to them and grumbled through every minute of the game.

Mick Tomlinson, the treasurer, who had nursed me, with a gentle mixture of wit and sarcasm, through those early days when I knew nothing and who had still acted as baby-sitter when I thought I knew it all.

The ladies who pretended not to notice when I pinched the odd pork pie and a scone. Northern Premier League clubs were rated on their pork pies and Matlock were always heading for promotion.

A cold March wind scuttled across the pitch and rippled a small pond in the penalty area until it lapped against the goalposts. Throughout the winter the pitch would be covered with either a foot of water

153

or six inches of snow. Football was a summer game in Matlock.

I had arrived one day to find the ground empty and the pitch flooded. The game had been abandoned and I was the only one who didn't know.

'Oh God!' The studio in Derby grumbled when I told them. *'We haven't got a programme – everything's off. Try and get an interview with Peter Swan.'*

The Matlock manager and ex-England centre half had long gone home and I left the phone and sat on the perimeter wall.

As I tried to think of an answer a small duck landed in the penalty area and swam in and out of the goalposts. He bobbed his head under the water and saluted me with his little feathered rear end.

'I can't find Peter Swan – but I'm going to interview a duck.'

'A what?'

He was the perfect professional. I hung my microphone over the edge of the wall and he swam over to me.

'Excuse me – but what do you think of the conditions today?'

'Quack.'

'So you think the game should never have been abandoned?'

'Quack.'

'If you had played today – what formation would you have adopted?'

'Quack – quack.'

'Really?'

'Quack.'

He was wonderful. Every time I stuck the microphone under his beak he came up with a different line in quacks – some were rather thoughtful with academic overtones, others were incisive, and his sparkling personality cut through the language barrier like a knife.

I tried to thank him properly, but he was a modest little duck and he swam away and pretended to examine the penalty spot. They played the interview four times during the afternoon and on each occasion he sounded better.

I don't know what he's doing now. I hope he moved on to better things – maybe he's with Manchester United. He certainly had the talent, but it all depends on the breaks you get in this life, doesn't it?

Only those who have had a meaningful relationship with a duck will understand the spring that came back into my step as I turned over the memories in my mind and walked back to the car.

On the way out of Matlock I passed the end of Gritstone Road once more and thought about my sink unit. It was a miserable old sink unit and well past its best and as for the cupboard, only the paint was holding the damned thing together. Anyone in their right mind would have thrown it out – I should have done it years ago.

I smiled at the way the incident had affected me and then the smile disappeared as I realized that I had visited my old home and not once had I thought of Diana.

I didn't know whether this was a good thing or a bad thing. There was a lot I didn't know.

Back in Chesterfield I let myself in through the kitchen door and tiptoed past the breadbin. The snores, first a rasp and then a fluted counterpoint, suggested that both cats were in residence and taking it in turns.

My mother sat on the settee watching television with her back to me. I waited – so many times I had said hello and then watched as she took off like a rocket. I didn't want a heart attack to come hard on the heels of the stroke.

155

I patted her on the shoulder, first gently and then once more, a little harder. She didn't move and my heart sank and then she coughed and shifted slightly. My heart climbed back up and fanned itself.

I went out of the house and stood in front of the French windows right in her line of vision. She looked up, her bifocals on the end of her nose, and stared straight through me.

A tap on the window might do it. I tapped and she looked over her shoulder and out towards the road.

This was silly. I went back in through the kitchen and pushed open the lounge door – then the phone rang in the hall.

'Come in,' shouted my mother.

I turned to answer the phone and it stopped.

'Come in – it's not locked,' she yelled. I went in, pushing the door closed behind me.

'You took your time – would you like a coffee?'

'I'd love one.'

'Please yourself, I'm having one – ouch!'

'What's the matter?'

'The doctor says I've got a frozen shoulder.' She slid a corner of her cardigan away to reveal a hot water-bottle strapped exactly where Long John Silver would have stood his parrot. No wonder I hadn't been able to get through with my Morse code.

'You're in the wars, aren't you, love – I'll make the coffee.'

I reached for the doorhandle and there wasn't one.

'Where's the doorhandle, Mum?'

'It's in that drawer over there – the one in the bureau.'

I tried the drawer.

'Where's the key?'

'It's in that drawer over there – the one in the wall cabinet.'

It was like breaking into a bank. The wrought-iron doorhandle had been wrapped in tissue paper, folded

156

into a polythene bag and then secured by several rubber bands.

I unwrapped it and opened the door. My mother watched me.

'You'll put it back when you've finished with it, won't you?'

I did put it back. I wrapped it up snugly in the tissue paper then dropped it into the polythene bag. My mother saw to the rubber bands – she wanted it done properly.

Before that I had tried to fix it back on the door.

'Where's your screwdriver, love?'

'Why?'

'I'll screw this back on.'

'No.'

The word came out sharp and hard with just a slight touch of panic about it and as she spoke she walked over and took the doorhandle from me.

'No.'

'All right.'

This needed treating with care. Something was wrong and I wasn't going to put it right by bullying her.

We watched television for most of the evening and every time I came back into the room with a drink I made a point of snicking the door behind me. This meant I had to go through the ritual of unwrapping the handle each time I went out again.

I tried to act as though this was what everyone did when they opened a door. I didn't ask why – I wanted her to tell me.

She watched me the first couple of times and said nothing. I extracted the handle with due formality on both occasions, very slowly and with great care.

The third time she stopped me as I opened the wall cabinet door for the key.

'Here – use these.'

From her overall pocket she produced a pair of pliers and handed them to me.

'It's a lot easier. You can turn that spindle thing with these, but they can't.'

She gave me a crafty look of triumph that was totally out of character – if she had been up on a stage I would have accused her of overacting. It was a wicked witch of a look, designed to carry its message to the dumbest kid in the audience.

'Who are *they*, Mum?'

That look again. Then she went back to the television and turned up the volume.

'Little devils,' she muttered.

No matter how I tried to draw her out she switched the conversation away from *them* with all the skill of a cabinet minister. She laced her bedtime cocoa with a dose of Buttercup Syrup.

'Well, I'm off to bed.'

With the exception of the bathroom doorknob all the handles had been removed and tucked away in cupboards and drawers. As I undressed I could hear her out on the landing, working away and grunting with exasperation. I could guess what she was doing. She knocked at my door and walked in.

'Could you give me a hand?'

She had managed to remove two of the three screws, but the third was made of sterner stuff and it was quite a while before I persuaded it to give itself up.

'Thank you – that's better. I shall sleep now.'

In the morning I arranged her Mother's Day flowers in a vase. I wasn't very good at it but I was far better than she was. After being handled by my mother, a bunch of flowers would have a startled look about them until the day they withered and died. It was as though they were in a state of shock.

She was thrilled with them. I took them up on a tray along with a cup of tea and a box of Thornton's chocolates. She sniffed each flower in turn and then insisted that Whisky and Horace do the same. The top layer of chocolates served as her breakfast and she left the card to last.

She was so pleased and excited that I had remembered and she opened the card as though it were the first time she had seen it.

'That's lovely.'

I hadn't really looked at it properly in the shop – she had taken all the responsibility out of my hands. It was only a few moments earlier that I had noticed the message.

She read the card over and over and then wet her thumb and rubbed out the price on the back.

'That's really lovely.'

She showed it to Whisky before standing it on her bedside table.

The message read, 'Congratulations on your retirement – from all your mates at work.'

Everything seemed to be back to normal.

Chapter 17

Aileen came back from posting her letters with a chip on her shoulder and a gleam in her eye.

'It's still there,' she shouted as she passed through the hall, 'I'm going to do something about it.'

'Mmmm,' I said or something rather similar, I can't remember exactly what it was but it seemed quite supportive at the time. I was working hard on the collection of my radio pieces and they were coming to life.

Every afternoon at four-thirty Aileen walked down to the post-box on the corner. It was a part of her self-sufficiency programme – she needed to prove, to others and to herself, that she could live a normal life without being wet nursed.

In the early days I tended to overdo it. I had been used to looking after a woman who needed me all her waking hours and I'd watched Aileen's every move.

'Here, give that to me – let me do it.'

'I'll see to that for you.'

Now I had the balance about right but it wasn't always easy. She had once crashed through a plate-glass window and the scar tissue left by 180 stitches ran from just over her left eye, across her scalp and down the full length of her back. I had traced it with my finger and shivered.

I put my head around her office door to find out what it was I had mmmm-ed at. She was on the phone.

'Just at the corner – yes. It must be all of four feet across and there's no warning, no cones or anything – anybody could fall in.'

It seemed that apologies were coming thick and fast at the other end and then a solution.

'Right – I'll be in.'

She put the phone down.

'What is it – that hole?'

'Yes – the council are sending some men out.'

She had told me last night about this hole. She didn't know how deep it was but it was right in the middle of the pavement and it was a wonder she hadn't fallen in. Some men had been working nearby – she'd mentioned it to them.

'Strange they haven't put cones round it.'

We went back to work until the bell rang. Two men stood on the doorstep and another waited on the lorry guarding an assortment of picks, shovels and cones.

'I'll show you.'

Aileen walked ahead of us, confident on her own territory.

'It's really dangerous.'

She stopped short of the corner and then picked her way carefully towards the edge of the hole.

'Look at that.'

The workmen looked at it and then they looked at one another. I took hold of Aileen's arm.

'It's a shadow, love. The shadow of a tree in the park.'

She said nothing – just stared at it and gingerly dipped her toe into its blackness. She stepped forward until she was standing in the middle of the shadow and then she turned round to face us.

'I wish it was a hole.'

As we walked back through the garden the dog from the downstairs flat was having a pre-tea-time crap on the lawn. I like to think that I can see the best in all creatures, human or otherwise, but in the case of the dog from the downstairs flat I made an exception.

161

It seemed that his only aim in life was to cover the entire western world with large brown torpedoes, starting with our lawn. Then under the cover of darkness he moved them about, placing them strategically along the path so that they would explode under some unsuspecting foot.

There's no doubt about it, he was a craftsman. When he put his mind to it he could manufacture the perfect croissant and dogs from all over Huddersfield came to admire his handiwork and learn the tricks of the trade.

His owners loved him and seemed reluctant to clean up his offerings; so they would lie there on the grass until they went white with age like eclairs that had spent far too long sunning themselves in a baker's window.

When he wasn't crapping he was scratching and right now he was doing both up against a post in the garden. The cat from the downstairs flat watched in disgust as his fellow lodger machine-tooled yet another work of art.

I hadn't seen that post before. An estate agent's sign dipped down towards the lawn as the dog massaged its rump.

'Aileen – it's for sale.'

'What is?'

'The downstairs flat – I'm going to buy it.'

I nipped upstairs for her binoculars and then we walked across the road to the park from where we could see the building as a whole.

I loved to see her use the binoculars. Often, when she heard the gate click, she would chart the caller's progress up the path and through the courtyard until they hesitated, just a couple of feet away from her.

The postman found it quite unnerving, and so did Aileen when at last she would lower the binoculars and find him peering in through the other end.

162

She only ever removed the cap from the left-eye piece – if I used them straight after her I went dizzy and fell over.

The house was a lovely, ugly old house – the Munsters would have felt at home here. We had often dreamt of restoring it to its former glory and now it seemed we had the chance.

It rose up four storeys above the park, a typical Yorkshire millowner's house – all solid stone and no nonsense.

'We'll have it just the way it was,' murmured Aileen from under the binoculars. I did a quick check in my head.

'We shall have eighteen rooms,' I told her.

'Well, there *are* two of us,' she said.

Aileen had been in the downstairs flat before but I hadn't and so we knocked at the door and asked if we could have a look round.

'I should tell you,' the owner said, 'that we have dry-rot in our bedroom floor, but I've already adjusted the price to account for that.'

At least he was being honest about it. But as soon as he opened the bedroom door I realized that he had little choice – the sweet, mushroomy scent of decay bent my nostrils back. If he didn't do something about it soon the dry-rot would have raced across the bedroom floor and be having breakfast in his kitchen. He would have to do a little more adjusting.

Back in Aileen's flat we rang Multiskill and asked them to carry out a survey for us.

'It could have spread even further than the bedroom.'

The man agreed with me.

'It could even be on its way up to you – it can travel through stone walls at about a metre a month.'

I told Aileen and she shuddered. Her study was directly over the bedroom. We felt like setting up a machine-gun post, ready to open fire the moment it popped its head up.

Later that night Nick rang from my mother's. Immediately I anticipated the worst.

'What's wrong?'

'Nothing – she's fine. I just thought I'd give you a ring, it's cheaper on her phone – you pay the bill.'

'Has she been acting strangely?'

'Yes – she always acts strangely.'

'I mean from usual – what about the doorknobs?'

'She's still wrapping them up, but now she keeps saying, "I'm daft, aren't I?" She's happy though – I've put her mind to rest about the cat.'

'Whisky?'

'She thought he was anorexic.'

'How come?'

He took a deep breath.

'She wanted to worm him so she had to find out how much he weighs but he wouldn't register on the scales. So – she weighed herself without the cat and then again holding the cat. That way she could take one away from the other and find out how heavy he was.'

'And?'

'She weighed the same both times so she was convinced he'd disappeared down to nothing.'

'What did you say?'

'I said that maybe he was holding his breath.'

I thought about that one.

'Yes?'

'She said that would make him heavier so I suggested he might be breathing out and she said yes, that would do it.'

'So she's stopped worrying?'

'Yes – she's upstairs now. She's put both Horace and Whisky on the scales and if she gets a reading she's going to divide by two.'

I could sit down later with a cup of tea and work all that out at my leisure.

'Have you been there long?'

'Since tea-time – four hours or so. She's all right apart from the doorknobs and the plugs.'

'What plugs?'

'In the sink and the bath – didn't you know about that?'

'No.'

'They have to be stuck in the plughole all the time so that whatever it is can't climb up.'

'That's a new one.'

'And the lavatory seat – it has to be down so they can't get in there.'

'Did she tell you what *they* are?'

'No – sort of gremlins, I suppose.'

'Is she frightened?'

'No – she's quite triumphant. She says she's got 'em licked.'

'I don't like it.'

'No, I know. But she's all right – I'll keep an eye on her, you just get settled over there. How are things?'

I told him about the flat and he was delighted.

'So you'll own the whole house between you and have a granny flat as well.'

'Yes – sort of.'

A granny flat. It brought to the surface a few half-thoughts I had been only too happy to keep submerged. What if my mother could no longer live on her own? What if she became senile?

Whilst I lived in Aileen's flat I couldn't take her in – it wouldn't be fair; but if I had my own house again . . . ?

My mother had taken in four of her sisters without a second thought and she couldn't stand the sight of two of them.

I loved her very much, but I had nursed Diana through fifteen years of pain and desperation and it had taken its toll – I couldn't do it again.

Anyway she loved living on her own. She would be all right – she had always said that she would never come and live with Diana and me.

'You have your own life, I wouldn't inflict that on you. I know what it's like – I'd rather go into a home.'

That's what she had said, I remembered it well. Memories can be very convenient at times.

The letter from the June Hall Literary Agency chased everything else from my mind.

The agency already represented Aileen's interests and she had recommended me. They didn't like taking on couples – if they had bad news for one they upset the other, but they would have a look anyway.

I had sent the first fifty pages of my book and now June Hall wrote to say that she would like to meet me – could I come to London?

I took the news very calmly. Just a quick somersault across the hall carpet before racing up the stairs and into the bedroom to tell Aileen. She took the news in her stride without any outward show of enthusiasm – but then she was still fast asleep.

A short stop halfway down the stairs to read the letter again and then into the kitchen where I jammed it up against the taps so that I could skim through it whilst I made her a cup of tea. It was just as hard to get an agent these days as it was a publisher.

I dried the letter out in front of the fire after it had fallen into the sink and then read it aloud to next door's cat who had popped in for a second breakfast and a look at the papers.

He was quite interested but nowhere near as excited as Aileen was after I had injected her third cup of tea straight into the vein.

166

We danced around the dining table and then I stood on a chair and read it to her once again. She said she was very proud of me and thought I should put some clothes on.

I stuck the letter behind the soap dispenser for a final check whilst I had a shower and then pinned it to the bookcase in my office – it's no good going overboard about these things.

As I drove down to London I turned the coming interview over a hundred times inside my head.

June Hall made no effort to hide her admiration as I flashed past Leicester Forest East where she compared me favourably with James Thurber, but by the time I pulled up at the Blue Boar for coffee she had hardened her attitude somewhat and was pulling the manuscript to pieces line by line, word by word.

She eased up on me slightly as I bobbed and ducked through the London traffic but she had already turned me into a nervous wreck and I hadn't met her yet.

When I did she was delightful and after introducing me to her colleagues she took me out to lunch.

'We can walk,' she said and I wondered where she would take me. Only a couple of Sundays ago I had read in a colour supplement that she had sold Clive Barker's latest novel to the States for something like a million dollars.

It would obviously be some watering hole where the literati gathered – I wondered if I would recognize any faces.

'Here we are,' she murmured and we walked into the Pizza Hut.

We sat at a table in the window and I talked too much, as I do when I'm nervous – about Diana and about our life together, the fun and the suffering, the hospitals, the hope and the helplessness of it all.

She listened and then patted my fifty pages of tarted-up radio scripts – all filleted for easy reading.

'So where's the pain?' she asked.

For over twelve years on the radio I had painted word-pictures in light colours to hide the reality, picking out the humour in pastel shades – never dipping into the black.

'If you can do it – you'll have a book,' she told me as we said goodbye.

Then she went off to bully some poor publisher and I drove home to write the pain.

Chapter 18

I cursed my new agent loud and often during the first few weeks. All the memories I had so carefully trussed up and pushed to the back of my mind began to wriggle free.

Every morning I had breakfast with Aileen and then went into my office to spend the day with Diana who seemed to come alive once more until I could write about her as though she were sitting beside me.

The book began to take shape and it wasn't the shape I had anticipated. As I wrote of her pain and frustration, of the weeks, months and years of suffering, the real woman began to set herself down on the pages and Diana would tell me, 'That's better – that's me. Don't let them think I'm a wimp.'

The joy began to merge with the misery and although the hours in the office often hurt as the pictures bounced back through my mind, for the first time in a long time I was sleeping at nights.

The nightmares were still frequent visitors, but now they had extended their repertoire and were not obsessed with drowning.

In the next room Aileen was putting the finishing touches to *Chapter of Innocence* and it was just one-thirty in the morning when she put her head round the door.

'Switch your intercom on.'

She loves gadgets. On her desk she has her computer, a printer, two phones and a closed circuit television for reading her scripts. There's a fax machine, a dictating machine, the Ansaphone and a tape recorder – sometimes I go in there and I can't find her.

When she saw the intercom she couldn't understand how we had ever managed without it. It was to become the hub of our communications centre.

'Feel like making a cup of tea?'

'Yes.'

'Lovely.'

Without the machine she would have had to walk at least three yards to ask me that.

Unfortunately my Amstrad had rejected it – the two just couldn't work together and so I had to switch the intercom off.

I switched it on again. Aileen buzzed and I answered.

'Hello?'

'Mr Longden?'

'Speaking.'

'I'VE FINISHED!'

We did a little dance around her office, shared a fluted champagne glass of Heineken lager and then I stood in silence as she ceremoniously printed out the three hundred and sixty-first page of her twenty-fifth novel. Then I went back to work – I was halfway down page forty-seven of my first.

She was too excited to sleep and so she roamed around the house sizing up walls and making plans as I worked at my desk. We had been the proud owners of the downstairs flat for some three days now but we had been too busy to think about it.

At a quarter past two I heard a steady thumping coming from the hallway. It could have been the sound of someone hitting a wall with a small hammer. I shot out to investigate and there was Aileen hitting the wall with a small hammer.

'I'm sure there must be a staircase behind here – it stands to reason.'

I suggested that perhaps it might be a good idea to remove all the pictures first and take the shades and bulbs from the wall-lights and then we rolled back the carpet and I fetched another hammer and joined in with her.

By three o'clock in the morning we had made a hole large enough to take the head and shoulders of a small woman with a flashlight in her mouth.

'Let me see first.'

She put her foot in my hands and I shoved the top half of her body through the hole.

'I can't see anything,' she muttered, chewing on the torch.

This was probably the only flaw in the plan and it was debatable which of us was the daftest for not anticipating it – but then it was her initiative and she deserved the honour of being the first to lead us over the top.

Her shoulders had to be threaded out of the hole, but it was only as I gently unscrewed her head to the left that the flashlight fell from her mouth.

We listened spellbound as we heard it crash to the floor on the other side of the wall, roll across bare floorboards and then thump steadily downhill on step after step after step.

We had our second dance of the evening, a much shorter one this time, a quick polka round the Chinese rug and then we were back with our hammers at the wall.

It continued to put up a good fight. These were breeze-blocks, a material unknown to the original builders, and together with Aileen's wild backswing they combined to form a rare challenge.

Within the hour we had carved out a hole the size of a serving hatch, just large enough for me to squeeze through. I dropped down on to a small landing and there, lit from underneath by a flashlight standing to attention on the bottom step, was a lovely winding staircase that had been hidden away for some forty-five years.

I picked my way carefully but the stairs were as solid as rock, not a creak or a groan. A single spider sat by the torch blinking at the light and trying to come to terms with his newly found freedom.

He didn't make a fuss of me. He just sat and stared as I examined the wall at the bottom. It seemed quite flimsy, definitely not breeze-blocks this one.

I put my shoulder to it and it gave under the pressure and so I nipped back uphill and then charged. The spider held his breath and then burst into silent applause as his hero smashed through a single sheet of hardboard and on out through the double doors of a clothes cupboard before tumbling head over heels into the downstairs flat.

A week later a team of builders turned up with bigger and better hammers and in no time at all the two flats became one very large house with eighteen very large rooms and still Aileen wasn't satisfied.

She had tasted success and so she prowled about the place, banging the walls with her little hammer. I followed her around filling in the dents with Polyfilla and tried to explain that the odds on finding another staircase were very small indeed.

Then one night we were down in the cellar when she turned and thumped the wall very hard – she liked to take walls by surprise. To my amazement a brick shot out leaving a hole about the size of a brick.

'Hang on.'

I stopped her as she hurled herself at the neat little hole.

'That could be the outside wall.'

When you meander down a winding staircase through four floors you lose all sense of direction. I poked the torch in the hole but all I could see were strange shapes and shadows, then a piece of string dangled in mid-air. I pulled it and a toilet flushed – I just hoped it was ours.

We loosened a few more bricks but it became obvious that this was a different proposition altogether. The spider in the staircase had become introspective in his isolation, a deep thinker who had kept the place nice and tidy. Down here they were drinking meths straight from the bottle, playing cards for money and swearing like troopers. No way was I going in there.

So the builders came back and in no time at all we had room nineteen, a pleasant little privy, all spick and span and smelling of Andrex. Multiskill came and took the dry rot away with them, leaving us freshly planed floorboards and a strange smell like that of a midwife's apron.

A coat of paint brought the bedroom back to life and I started on the drawing room. It was like decorating an aircraft hangar with an embossed ceiling. The pelmets were fifteen feet across and two feet deep in carved wood with swirls and squiggles that defy description. The only consolation was that they were so far from the ground no-one was likely to point at them and say 'You've missed a bit.'

I made the mistake of describing the ceiling to Aileen.

'It's amazing – hundreds of squares and circles, each with a tiny rose.'

She thought that sounded lovely and came back a few moments later with an idea.

'Wouldn't it be wonderful if the roses were all picked out in pink?'

I handed her a hammer and sent her off in search of walls.

It was all a bit of a lick and a promise, but we had put our mark on the place and it was clean and fresh once more. My mother would be happy here.

The guilt had been hammering away at me. We had all this room and she needed looking after. She would have a flat here that was bigger than her own house. She could be independent and at the same time I could keep an eye on her.

It was the perfect solution – there was even a built-in wall cupboard where she could keep all the doorhandles.

I talked it over with Aileen and she said fine – if that was what I wanted and I said it was.

But it wasn't really. I had been badly bruised by the last fifteen years and more than anything I wanted to start my new life free to find out about myself – to see how far I could go. I had walked at Diana's pace for so long and been happy to do so, but now I wanted to run.

When I went to see my mother in Chesterfield it was like dipping my toe in the past – I could always fly back to the future. To have her here, in failing health, would mean that it had all caught up with me again.

I was determined to be honest with myself, but I can't say it gave me any feeling of pride.

At least it would cut out all this driving down the M1. Three times a week until I was now on first-name terms with every cone between junctions thirty-eight and twenty-nine.

I could hear my mother singing as I walked down the path. She was in a modern mood this morning, treating the immediate neighbourhood to the latest hits of Miss Gracie Fields and I waited outside the door and listened carefully to see if I could make out the words. Yes – she was doing well.

She moved up a couple of notches as she prepared to belt out her famous version of 'Sally' and both Horace and Whisky came out of the kitchen and sat on the path until she had worked it out of her system. Then, as she slipped down a gear or so for her Stanley Holloway impression, they walked back in and I followed them.

She was hand-washing her lace curtains in the sink but she quickly reached for the towel when she saw me.

'Come and look at this.'

She fell down on to her knees by the side of the fridge and I knelt down beside her.

'It's for Horace.'

Where Whisky's breadbin had stood alone for years there were now two breadbins, butting up to one another like bungalows on a new estate.

'It's the one I was using.'

Horace came and sat beside me and I told him I thought it was very nice. She had grassed the area with an offcut from the back bedroom carpet and the cat litter tray took up the far left-hand corner whilst two bowls, one plain white and the other marked 'Dog', were tucked up against the fridge on the right.

'It's only right he should have his own breadbin.'

'Which is his bowl?'

'The one with his name on it.'

Whisky wasn't so sure about all this – he didn't like changes. For years he'd had a view and now they were building all around him.

My mother climbed to her feet via a chair and the kitchen table, her right arm still seemed to be weak.

'I'm having trouble with this though,' she said, pointing to a brand-new breadbin on the table. 'The lid won't stay up.'

It was almost like ours, green and white with a roll-top lid that folded back inside itself, but this one had 'Daerb' written across the front in what looked like Russian.

'We've got one like that.'

'Then you'll know about them.'

I turned it the right way up.

'Try it now.'

175

She did and it worked perfectly. She was delighted and flipped the lid open and shut several times.

'Thank you, love – you always were good with your hands.'

Whisky jumped up to see what all the fuss was about and she showed him.

'Look at that, Whisky,' she said to the cat, 'your brother's mended it.'

I did a few other jobs around the house, nothing too difficult. She was having trouble with the Hoover.

'It's blowing back at me.'

She never emptied the bag and it stood in the hall pregnant with fluff and gravel.

'It's never been right since we had that snow in January.'

I didn't want to explore the significance of that remark, but I knew it would haunt me for ever if I let it go.

'You haven't been Hoovering snow off the path?'

She was quite indignant.

'Course I haven't – just the windowsills and that bit round the French windows.'

I nipped out for fish and chips at lunchtime while my mother warmed the plates and set up the salt and vinegar, then we sat round the fire and tucked in.

'The chip shop's changed hands,' I told her.

'I know.'

'It's Chinese now.'

'I've seen them. They've got a baby – he's Chinese as well.'

It was a good lunch, spiced with intelligent conversation and finished off with two iced cherry buns from Henstocks.

I made us both a mug of tea and sank back in the armchair with a cigarette. A silver frame on the mantelpiece caught my eye and there was my father looking down at me.

'Where's that from?'

'He's been in the airing cupboard – he's a bit warped, but I thought I'd give him a run.'

I wondered how I could have been so frightened of a man who was the spitting image of Stan Laurel. I remembered sitting by the fire like this with my mother when I was only nine. She had opened an envelope and taken out a letter. I waited while she read it slowly and then she put it down.

I knew then that he had been killed in action. John Taylor hadn't been in school yesterday and the teacher told us why.

My mother had reached out and poked the fire then leant over towards me.

'I want you to be brave, Deric.'

I said I would be.

'Only he's coming home for good this weekend.'

A ripple of applause brought me back to the present as my mother switched on the television.

'It's skating – I don't know how they stand up.'

I wanted to talk about the flat and I wished I had done it earlier. It wasn't easy to hold her attention at the best of times but the television always took some beating.

'You know the flat I was talking about – the one on the ground floor?'

'Yes.'

It was a floating yes. The sort of yes that is always accompanied by a pair of eyes that drift away from you. This time back to the television.

'Well, I've bought it.'

'You what?'

That got her. It was property, you see – bricks and mortar. To hell with the skating.

'I've bought it.'

177

'Well done.'

She had always enjoyed property. The times she had pleaded with my father, *'Buy it, Fred – not for the house, for that field at the back.'*

He hadn't. Not because it was a bad idea but simply because she had suggested it – she was a woman, what did she know? Someone else built twenty-four houses on that field.

When he did have a go years later she implored him, *'Keep one in every four, Fred – don't sell them all. They'll be worth a fortune one day.'*

He hadn't and they doubled in value within the year. They were worth £80,000 each today. She loved property and she came alive.

'Right – now then. A big house like that, it'll be worth four times as much in three years' time. But for now, rent the flat out and get some money back – you could get £100 a week for that. £100 a week for three years, that's . . . '

'I don't want to do that.' I must have sounded like my father. 'I want you to move in.'

'I couldn't afford that.'

'I don't want you to pay anything.'

'Are you serious?'

'Yes.'

She turned away to the television. A fourteen-year-old Canadian girl whirled around the rink to the sound of Michael Jackson singing 'Ben'.

'Mum.'

She watched the girl cut patterns in the ice as she spun and swayed through her routine.

'It's a lovely flat. You would be quite independent and there's a park across the road and shops nearby. You'd have all the money from this place and I'll be just upstairs if you need me. I wouldn't interfere.'

She never took her eyes from the television.

'I told you I'd never come and live with you.'

'This is different. It would be your own place.'

'It doesn't work.'

'You took everybody in.'

'That's how I know it doesn't work – I ended up hating Jessie.' She turned back to face me. 'I don't want to leave here – my friends are here. I've only ever had four houses, all within a mile of where I was born.'

'You could have another stroke.'

'I've thought of that.'

'And?'

'I've found a place. It's called Springbank House – it seems very nice.'

'There's no need.'

She plucked Whisky from the hearthrug and sat him on her knee.

'There's every need. You've had enough – more than enough. Tell me something.'

'What?'

'When the time comes will you move in with Sally or Nick?'

'You wouldn't be moving in with me.'

The Canadian girl came to a halt in the middle of the ring and took her bow.

'She was never singing that – her lips never moved.'

'No – it was Michael Jackson on a record. She was just skating to it.'

'They're not allowed to do that these days – I read it somewhere.' She stroked Whisky and nudged Horace with her foot. 'Just look after these two if anything happens and stop worrying about me – I'll be all right.'

We sat in silence for a while.

'Promise me you'll think about it,' I asked her.

'I've thought about it.'

'What about the gremlins? You know, the door-handles and the plugs?'

She slipped the cat in the chair behind her and stood up.

'Nick says they can't do any harm.'

'He's right.'

'So there's nothing to worry about, is there?'

I seemed to have played my cards wrong. She had all the aces – or was it that I wasn't trying hard enough to win.

She picked up the photo of my father and smiled.

'He looked a duck in plus-fours, didn't he?'

I held my hand out and she handed the picture to me.

'I do appreciate it, love – I really do, but I'd rather stop here. Let's have a cup of tea.'

She went out in to the kitchen and the two cats and I followed in single file.

'What did you have on the mantelpiece before this? I can't remember.'

She switched on the kettle and took another two iced cherry buns from her new breadbin.

'It was you in your white angora bonnet and your little white bootees. I'd had it up there for fifty years and I was sick to bloody death of it.'

Chapter 19

Watching Aileen read the *Huddersfield Examiner* was a painful business. Every night she scanned the 'For Sale' column, the 'Under a Tenner' column and 'Lost and Found'.

'Lost and Found' depressed her terribly. She would worry herself sick over puppy George who, with his one black eye and his limp, had last been seen chasing a motor bike up Lindley Road. She would listen to the rain battering against the window.

'Poor little devil – he'll be soaked.'

I found it painful to watch her. She wore a special pair of monocular spectacles for the occasion, the right lens boarded up, the left projecting like a telescope towards the close circuit television which had already blown up each letter to a height of two inches.

Newspapers aren't meant to be read under a close circuit television, the pages would screw up and she would lose her place.

'Damn.'

'Shall I read it to you?'

'I'm all right.'

This nightly scanning of the small ads was a recent innovation, introduced since we had swallowed up the rooms downstairs. We had rooms until they were coming out of our ears – what we didn't have was furniture.

'There's one here. *"Green dralon three-piece suite with one chair"*.'

'That's only two pieces.'

'I've lost it again. Damn it – it was the one under twenty-one tons of grey roofing slates.'

'It's a wonder they ever found it.'

Eventually her eye would tell her that it wanted to take a nap now and I would move into the driving seat. I was quicker, I could scan and be selective and miss out those I thought she might find interesting.

I loathed turning up on a strange doorstep and asking if we could have a look at their three-piece suite. Aileen could only see a vague outline.

'What sort of condition is it in, Deric?'

The rather nice couple would wait anxiously to hear what I had to say. The baby would take a break from strangling the cat and the four of them would lean forward, hanging on my every word.

How could I tell her that there was a half-eaten Farley's Rusk sticking out from behind a cushion, that the cat had used it as a scratching post and anyway I wouldn't fancy a hard-boiled egg if it came from this house?

'I think it would clash with our carpet.'

That became our secret password. If I said it would clash with our carpet we moved on. It didn't work so well with chest freezers and standard lamps.

Whilst I severely edited the For Sale columns I took great pleasure in fleshing out the Lost and Found.

I could skip such items as *'Lost – half-Persian kitten.'* Losing a whole kitten was one thing, losing half of one amounted to nothing short of carelessness and it would only bring a tear to Aileen's long-suffering eyes.

But with a little imagination I could make her night as I sat bolt upright and crackled the paper.

'Listen to this.'

'What?'

'You remember George from last night? The puppy with the one black eye and the limp?'

'Yes.'

'They've found him.'

'Where?'

'On Lindley Moor. Somebody had taken him in and fed him and given him a bed for the night. They say he's as right as rain and they want to thank the people who looked after him.'

'It says all that?'

'Yes.'

'Oh, that's wonderful.'

For a moment there I thought I had gone over the top, but I seemed to have got away with it and Aileen's broad smile was reward enough for my sins.

I just hoped that George would forgive me and that one day soon he would arrive home again safe and sound.

We had bought some bits and pieces, a table, four chairs and a sideboard, from a legitimate shop in town where a young man unnerved me by calling me sir thirty-five times in as many minutes, but we had much greater success in those junk-shops where they hadn't called anybody sir for the last thirty-five years.

For £40 we bought an enormous settee that could have come straight from Chatsworth House and for £45 a chandelier so upmarket that, had it been able to talk, it wouldn't have had anything to do with the likes of us.

We became junk-shop junkies and began to study form. I was in charge of transport and quality control. Aileen was the wheeler-dealer and chief sniffer-out. The larger the item, the cheaper it came.

'You see – nobody has houses big enough for this stuff these days.'

'That's true.'

'What are you going to do with it then?'

'It's for a church.'

Aileen soon discovered that she was a graduate of the Arthur Daly school of haggling and her strongest asset was the fact that she couldn't see the look of pain as it passed over the junk-shop owner's face. I could and so I always waited outside and smoked a furtive fag, not wishing to witness the distressing scene.

As we toured the junk shops of Yorkshire it seemed they all had the same settee standing outside on the pavement.

One week it would be uncut moquette in bright orange, the next a dark brown vinyl-leather with wooden arms that was once light fawn when it proudly wore its original price ticket back in 1968. A week later they would switch back again.

I had a funny feeling that the moment we left, two men with a Reliant Robin van would shove the settee in the back and race round to the next shop on our itinerary. When we arrived – there it would be, standing on the pavement.

Only the price ever changed, never the settee. And piled high beside it would be several Hoovers vintage 1948, a coffee table which flared up at each end as though it had been designed to take off at high speed and another coffee table, this time with screw-in legs all spindly with brass ferrules on the business end.

On the coffee table there would be a portable radio that was slightly heavier than the settee, its stations marked *Home Service*, *Light Programme* and *Hilversum*.

It was like taking a trip back into my youth and I promised Aileen that one day, if she was very good, I would buy her a Playtex circle-stitched bra and a girdle with living panels that breathed.

*   *   *

Our favourite shop was Mrs Singh's Sundal Corner. It was within small-object-carrying distance of the house and if Mrs Singh hadn't got what we wanted she would find it for us.

She found paintings, one very valuable, and odd items of furniture that decorated the house until we were taking stuff for her to sell.

I liked Mrs Singh, and when Aileen haggled with her I went across the road to smoke my furtive fag, browsing in the chemist's window until it was all over.

Having polished off the Lost and Found I moved on to the sports pages, but Aileen wasn't letting me off the hook.

'I've marked one in Under a Tenner.'

That spelt trouble and I turned back to see what I was in for but before I could find it – 'I've put a red cross – it's a bedhead in wrought iron – it might match the one in the small bedroom.'

I found it.

'I'll pop round in the morning.'

'It might be gone.'

'I'll ring them.'

'There isn't a phone number.'

'I'll go now.'

'I should.'

I could be very firm when I wanted to be.

I was still feeling my way around Huddersfield but I knew this little village quite well, we had had a pub lunch there.

'Take the paper with you.'

'I can remember that.'

'Take it anyway.'

'No need.'

What the hell was the address? Her name was Mrs Arrowsmith, I knew that. The name of the road had something to do with trees, or was it battles?

It was number four, I remembered now, that was it, number four. Or was it number seven? Sod it.

In front of me, on what passed for a main street, an old man walked his dog. He moved as though he had just had his zimmer-frame pinched out from under him and he hadn't realized it yet.

The dog waddled along, keeping two yards ahead, and yet at the same time managing to give the impression that it was the slower of the two. It was that rare breed, the village dog, and the twentieth century had passed him by.

The old man would know Mrs Arrowsmith. He would know everyone in the village and if he didn't, the dog would.

I tucked the car into the kerb and walked up behind them.

'Excuse me.'

The old man stopped and the dog didn't.

'Yes?'

'I'm looking for a Mrs Arrowsmith.'

'Are you now?'

He looked over his shoulder and then backed up until he was able to lower himself down on a garden wall. He shuffled until he was comfy and then stared at the pavement, conjuring pictures out of the wet slabs.

'We've got three. There's Mrs Arrowsmith wi' one leg, there's young Mrs Arrowsmith up at the farm and then there's Mrs Arrowsmith what has the house on Lupin Lane.'

'That's it – that's the one.' I remembered now – I knew it had something to do with trees or battles. The old man smiled.

'Oh, you'll like Mrs Arrowsmith – she's a lovely lady.'

Away in the distance the dog stopped and turned round to face us. He had been lost in his own thoughts for a while and look what happened when he wasn't concentrating. He sat down and glared at us.

'Oh no – not again. Another thirty minutes with nothing to do but sit down and lick my bum.'

The old man pointed down the road and the dog frowned at him, then turned to see what it was he had missed.

'Go down there and first on your left, then first left again and that's Lupin Lane. There's only five houses, but they're big 'uns. Mrs Arrowsmith's is the last but one.'

'Thank you very much – I appreciate it. Tell your dog I'm sorry for keeping him.'

He glanced towards the dog, who still hadn't worked out what it was he'd been pointing at, and gave a fond smile.

'Old Lewis. He should have been dead years ago, but he's stubborn – he's waiting for me.'

I turned to go but he hadn't finished with me yet.

'A word of warning, young man. Mrs Arrowsmith lives with her sister and they haven't spoken a word for the last twenty years. When they hear you knock at the door they'll both answer it. Mrs Arrowsmith is the one as smells of chips.'

It was an enormous house with a tiny front door that cowered under a porch. The garden had invaded the path and rose trees bent over at right angles as though they were trying to look up my trousers.

I rang the bell and nothing happened. Then the door was wrenched open and two old ladies stood there with their eyebrows raised enquiringly. One of them was breathing heavily as though she had had all on to make it a draw.

I sniffed the air and there was a smell of chips you could have cut with a vinegar bottle. I turned to address the lady on my left.

'Mrs Arrowsmith?'

'Yes?'

'I've come about the bedhead.'

The sister's face fell in disappointment, but Mrs Arrowsmith beamed.

'Just a minute.'

They both disappeared leaving the door wide open and I examined the hall while I waited. There was a shabby feel about the place, but it was neat and tidy and the furniture was straight out of *A Man For All Seasons*.

From the centre of the hall rose a huge staircase and right down the middle of the wide steps, as straight as a die, ran an inch wide line, chalked on the frayed carpet. It dropped off the bottom stair and then dissected the hall, coming to a halt at the doorstep under my feet.

' . . . *they haven't spoken a word for the last twenty years.*'

That's what it would be. 'This is my half and that's yours.' It seemed a very sad state of affairs and I bent down to examine the dividing line.

It wasn't chalk – it was dust. They must have each Hoovered their own half for goodness knows how long, but they'd be damned if they were going to go over on to her half.

There was a banging of doors and Mrs Arrowsmith appeared holding a bedhead. A split second later, the sister appeared at her elbow.

'That's perfect – that's just what I wanted.'

I handed over a £5 note.

'I only said £4.99.'

'That's all right.'

'Oh – thank you.'

The sister stared at the ceiling.

188

'I never take a penny that's not due to me.'

'Just a minute.'

Mrs Arrowsmith was off like a rabbit leaving only an invisible cloud of chip fat to keep her sister company. She reappeared as if by magic holding a penny in her hand.

'There you are.'

Aileen was watching a play on television when I arrived home. She was curled up on the floor with her hip up against the video and her nose pressed against the screen.

There must be a sex scene in the offing. Mostly she just listened to television, the visual aspect being completely lost on her. But let the dialogue get a little randy and she was down on the floor with her nose in amongst the static.

Her children played a game with her. They had it down to a fine art and I had watched a demonstration at Christmas.

Paul casually glanced across at the screen.

'Just look at those two.'

Aileen came to life.

'What? Are they in bed?'

She shuffled on to her bottom and edged up to the screen.

'Don't look, Mum – it's disgusting.' Annie told her with just the right amount of frost in her voice.

'What is?'

She was desperately trying to focus on the blurred screen and Paul added to her frustration.

'That's clever – I'd never have thought of trying that.'

'Trying what? What's he doing?'

Annie put her out of her misery.

'He's balancing the egg between his feet, Mum.'

Aileen had her back to the bird as it waddled off down the beach – she was in amongst her kids with a cushion and her strike rate was remarkable for a woman who couldn't see a penguin when it was standing on the end of her nose.

She hadn't heard me come in and I crept upstairs to try out the bedhead – it would be a surprise.

It was just like the one on the other bed and I was quite pleased with myself as I went back down to join her.

'You're back – this looks good. Tell me what's happening.'

I tried. I tried very hard, but the better the play the more difficult it is to keep up a running commentary. So much is said through body language and by a sideways glance.

'But he said he loved her.'

'Yes – but he gave her a funny look when he said it.'

'I'm fed up with this.'

The lousier the movie the easier it was for her. The old 'B' pictures were the best. They spelt it out.

I'm going to shoot you with this Smith and Wesson revolver I'm holding in my left hand.'

'Look out – the rope's fraying and it's a thousand-feet drop on to those rocks down there. But wait – who's that crawling along the parapet? My God, it's Louis.'

Three cheers for Louis. That sort of film she could handle and we would sit on the floor together and boo the villain.

'Did you get the bedhead?'

I wiped a black smut from the end of her nose – I must dust that television.

'Yes – I've fixed it.'

She went upstairs to have a look and I moved nearer to the screen, the play was hotting up again.

When she came back down she was in her dressing gown, ready for bed and looking far more desirable than the woman in the play.

I switched off the set – perhaps an early night, I thought. She sat at her desk and crossed her legs. Yes, an early night seemed a very good idea.

'I like the bedhead,' she said. 'It fits in perfectly.'

'Yes, I was pleased.'

She switched out the light above her desk and stood up.

'Have you had any supper?'

'No – why?'

'I just wondered. That back bedroom smells of chips.'

Chapter 20

My mother sat up in bed and nibbled at the edges of her sandwich. Then for the umpteenth time she parted the two slices of bread and had a peep inside.

'What did you say it was?'

'Prawn and mayonnaise.'

'You don't put prawns in a sandwich.'

'Marks & Spencer do – it's nice. Try it.'

She had run out of edges to nibble at and so she took a tentative bite.

'Well?'

'I've never been very keen on seafood, apart from fish.'

'You eat crab and lobster.'

'And those.'

'You like cockles and mussels.'

'I like shrimps as well.'

'There you are, then.'

She took another bite, a more confident bite this time and then another.

'This is nice – it's just seafood I'm not fond of.'

I had been surprised to find her in bed. I remembered her being tucked up for a couple of days once with pneumonia and for just over a week when she was in traction, but unless somebody strapped her down, five hours a night were usually more than enough for her.

Yet here she was with a fresh bottle of Buttercup Syrup by her side and her portable television on the bedside table looking for all the world as though she were here for the duration.

'What's wrong?'

'Nothing.'

Her eyes wandered over to the small screen as several teenage girls combined in an orgasmic screech.

'That's John Lloyd. It's no good them shouting – he's married to Tracey Austin.'

'Chrissie Evert.'

She leant closer to the set and screwed up her eyes for sharp focus.

'No, it's John Lloyd – they look a lot alike.'

She asked me to feed the cats but I could only find Whisky. Horace must be over at the allotments – he was running out of voles around here and was having to travel further afield to enjoy his manly pursuits. Mouse-stretching seemed to be the latest craze.

There was a can already open on the draining-board and so I pulled out the cutlery drawer for a spoon. It was almost empty – there was a single spoon, a knife and a fork and that was all.

Last week it had been full. She had loads of stuff, none of it matching as over the years knives and forks had been thrown away in the rubbish bin along with food from the plates, but there had been enough bits and pieces in there to ensure that it had to be shuffled about before the drawer would shut.

So where was it all? I combed the kitchen cupboards and found nothing and then I had an idea.

I took the key from the wall cabinet in the lounge and unlocked the bureau and there alongside the doorhandles and a single knob from the bathroom, all wrapped up in greaseproof paper and secured in polythene bags by rubber bands, were her knives and her forks and her spoons.

I checked up on the kitchen sink to see if she still kept the plug in place and sure enough it had been pressed firmly home to harbour three or four inches of clear water.

193

In the bathroom the story was the same. In both the bath and sink the plugs had been pushed tight and a few inches of water lapped around the chain.

The toilet seat was down and the weighing scales placed on top. On the scales stood a large brass duck – it weighed just under 4 lbs.

She was having a nap when I went back in to the bedroom and so I sat on the covers and read a story from her *People's Friend* very softly into Whisky's ear.

The young girl who worked as a maid in the Scottish castle seemed to be having a rough time. She was in love with the laird's son and there was no doubt about it, he fancied her like mad. But deep down they both knew that his family would have nothing to do with a serving wench.

Then just as she was packing her bags to make life easier for him a letter came from a solicitor, and would you believe it, she was actually the long-lost daughter of the laird's best friend and not only that, she had a bob or two waiting for her in Edinburgh.

Whisky was just as pleased as I was at the outcome, we both loved a happy ending and hoped that we could resolve my mother's problems as neatly as that.

Whisky saw something interesting by the skirting board and jumped off the bed to investigate. My mother woke up as he thumped down on to the floor.

'What time is it?'

'Twenty to three.'

'I'm missing Wimbledon.'

She switched on the television and reached for her glasses and the Buttercup Syrup.

'What are you frightened of, Mum?'

She shook her head.

'Nothing.'

'Then why all this business of the doorhandles?'

She paused, the bottle in one hand, the spoon in the other and looked very lost.

'And why have you wrapped up everything from the knife drawer?'

'I'm daft, aren't I?'

'No. You're not daft. What's worrying you?'

She waved the spoon at me and then she turned it in her hand until she was holding it like a dagger.

'They could stab me with them,' she whispered.

'Who could?'

'They could.'

'How would they get in?'

'How they always get in.'

I kept quiet and she had to fill the silence.

'Up the pipes and down the taps and in up the lavatory. They push the seat up.'

'They're only small, then?'

'Some are.'

'How could they reach the doorhandles?'

'Some aren't.'

She lay back on her pillow, her eyes searching the ceiling rather than take on mine.

'Have you seen one?'

She nodded and turned to stare out of the window.

'What was it like?'

I had to wait for the answer, it was a long time coming.

'It was black like a slug, all slimy and it came up through the plughole. It was watching me.'

'What did you do?'

'I hit it.'

'Did you kill it?'

'No.'

'What happened to it?'

'It's still here – in the house.'

She sat up straight, then she leant in close to me and I could feel her body stiffen.

'That's the trouble, you see. If I make it so *they* can't get in . . . '

Her eyes faded and then her body slumped as though it were all so hopeless.

' . . . then, I've made it so *he* can't get out. I just don't know what to do.'

I moved up the bed and put my arms around her and she hung on tight for a moment or so and then she broke away and gave me a great big smile.

'Have you seen what I've done?'

'What?'

'The water – in the bath.'

'Yes.'

'They're going to have a shock when they push that plug up, aren't they?'

She laughed. 'Serves the little devils right.'

She glanced across at Whisky who was still having a rare old game on the carpet. 'Stop him, will you.'

'What's he doing?'

'He's got my sticky tape.'

The cat was in a rare old mess. He had yards of Sellotape wrapped all around him and he was beginning to panic. What had started out as a bit of fun had got completely out of hand. I grabbed hold of him and began unwinding.

It was round his stomach and under his legs and the more he struggled the worse it became. I had to stretch it and then pull his head through until he broke free and ran from the room.

I gathered it all up into a ball but there was even more of it than I had imagined. The end seemed to be behind the dressing table and then I realized that it ran right around the room.

I looked up at my mother for an explanation.

'That's another way they get in – between the skirting board and the carpet. I've done all the house.'

This time it was as though a different woman was saying the words. As though sticking Sellotape all around the skirting boards was the most normal thing in the world. Everybody did it – like lagging the hot water tank or insulating the loft.

She was totally in control of herself once more. This was her house and she did what she wanted.

Over on the bedside table Dan Maskell was working himself up into restrained frenzy and she leant over and switched up the volume.

'Look, I'm missing my Wimbledon. Do me a favour, love, I could murder a cup of tea.'

And just like that it was, as though the last ten minutes had never happened.

I went down to the kitchen. What on earth was I going to do about this? See a doctor obviously and then she had better come home with me.

I switched on the tap to fill the kettle and nothing happened, I gave it another half turn and all hell was let loose. A jet of water hit the side of the kettle at 40 miles an hour and I was soaked to the skin. I switched the tap off and reached for the towel.

It must have been an air lock in the pipe. I filled the kettle again, slowly this time and then I saw the plug of paper floating in the sink. It had been screwed up carefully into a ball – I wonder?

I poked my little finger up the hot tap and there was another. I pushed the first plug back up the cold tap and made sure there was still a good 4 inches of water in the sink.

She seemed her old self as she sat up in bed and gave me a ball-by-ball commentary on the tennis. The little screen on the portable television had a dull, greenish cast about it.

'Have you noticed, the screen's all green.'

She looked at me as though I were two planks short of a load.

'It's Wimbledon.'

'Yes – but it's a black-and-white television.'

'Is it?'

The picture quality was awful. Two ghostlike figures roamed either side of a net that would have been better employed for trawling mackerel, and in their hands they held deformed snow-shoes. Since they didn't appear to have a ball it made very little difference to the game.

'Do you mind if I twiddle with the knobs?'

'As long as you don't ruin the picture.'

I twiddled and the screen went blank. The ghosts disappeared and all that was left was a little white spot in the middle. If only I could get the players back they could play with that.

'You've made it worse.'

'At least it's not green any more.'

'I liked it green – especially when it's Wimbledon.'

I twiddled on and the players reappeared, slightly clearer this time but still wavy and ethereal – a bit like Bendy toys.

'That's perfect,' she said, 'that's better than it's been for years. I didn't know you knew anything about television?'

'Just a little,' I said modestly as I watched John Lloyd bounce nothing three times before serving into the net.

The doorbell rang and the two copper tubes were still bouncing against the wall as I walked down the stairs. The surgery had said the doctor would call in on his way to work but this wasn't him, the figure on the other side of the glass door was slight and feminine.

'Sorry to bother you but your mother usually walks down to the shops about this time, only I should stop her if I were you.'

What on earth had she been up to?

'Only there's a cat been run over outside and it's ever such a mess and it'll only upset her.'

She turned to walk away and then stopped.

'It isn't your Whisky. It's been knocked about something terrible, but I could see it wasn't him.'

'No, Whisky's inside – but thank you for letting me know.'

I knew it had to be Horace. Poor old Horace, he was just beginning to look cared for. His coat had taken on a vigorous, healthy feel to it and he was proud of his cod-in-butter-sauce sheen.

He had filled out and developed the sort of confidence that comes only with belonging. He was still as ugly as sin, but he had begun to wear it like a badge, a gangster gone respectable.

We couldn't have him lying out there in the road and so I pulled a dustbin liner and a pair of gardening gloves from under the sink and went out to tidy him up.

I wasn't looking forward to this. I tend to become all brisk and workmanlike when there's a rotten job to be done, I put my mind on hold until it's all over but I could have done without this.

It was Horace all right. He was lying in the gutter and I pulled the gloves on as I walked towards him, telling my brain not to take any notice of what my eyes were about to see.

'It's ever such a mess and it'll only upset her.'

There wasn't a mark on him. It must have been a glancing blow and he couldn't have known much about it, there was no blood and there were no obvious breaks – he might have been asleep there in the gutter.

His head lay propped on the pavement as though it were a pillow and the tattered remains of his left ear stood out pink against his black fur, as did the one nostril that had battled on so gamely without a partner.

'It's been knocked about something terrible.'

Poor old Horace – he always looked like this. I tucked the dustbin liner under my arm and shoved the gloves back in my pocket, they would be the final insult.

I picked him up and carried him in as though I were taking him for his tea. Come on, old son – somebody loved you.

Chapter 21

I buried Horace in a corner of the garden by the lilac tree. He would have liked that. With Whisky cheering him on from the safety of the kitchen window he had mugged over 75 per cent of his victims from that very spot.

Since my mother was sure that he originally came from a good home and that somebody would be 'missing him', I toyed with the idea of letting her think he had just nipped back for his toothbrush and then decided to stay on for a while.

In the end I told her the 'truth', which was that I had found him lying in a patch of sunshine on the shed roof. He had a smile on his face and at first I thought he was merely asleep. He obviously hadn't suffered.

She took the news badly but then, after a good cry, she began to look on the positive side.

'He was very happy these last few months, wasn't he?'

'Very.'

'He knew we loved him.'

'I'm sure he did.'

'He was filling out – he was a handsome cat, wasn't he?'

'What would you like for your tea?'

She looked out of the back bedroom window at the lilac tree and although I am sure she would have preferred full military honours and a brass band, she was happy that he was there.

'Everything's so quick these days. We used to lay them out in the front room so people could visit.'

'Not cats though.'

'No, not cats.'

She went into the bathroom for a wash and I waited briefly at the door to see if she would be all right.

She pulled a plug of paper from the tap, emptied the sink and began to fill it again with hot water. I wondered if we had laid the gremlins to rest as well.

She looked over her shoulder at me.

'When I heard that woman at the door tell you a cat had been run over outside, I thought it was going to be Horace.'

'Did you?'

'Yes.'

'So did I, to be honest.'

She turned and smiled a smile at me that had eighty-odd years of wisdom all wrapped up in it.

'I'm glad it wasn't.'

'So was I.'

'Now push off – I'm going to have a good stand-up wash.'

We all sat and had our tea by the fire. Whisky had cod in butter sauce in a dish on the hearth and my mother had cod in butter sauce on a tray on her knee. I had cod in parsley sauce on sufferance, but at least it made my mother happy.

'I am glad – I've had that in the fridge for months. Whisky won't touch it, he doesn't like the green bits.'

The green bits were parsley, but I still didn't fancy it and so I moved it around the plate several times until it was about half the original size, then smuggled it out into the kitchen while Whisky chased a small piece of cod up and down the fireplace. When I returned he was licking the last of his sauce off a poker and my mother had dropped off to sleep.

The doctor had stepped up her medication and we would have to wait to see if it had any effect. He already knew about the gremlins and I had filled him in on their recent escapades before she came downstairs all freshly scrubbed and looking ten years younger.

'*You'll have a shock when you see her – she looks ten years older.*'

When he asked her about the gremlins she didn't know what he was talking about at first.

'*They were threatening you, Mrs Longden.*'

'*Were they?*'

'*They came up the plugholes.*'

'*Oh yes – Deric told me about them.*'

This always seemed to happen to me. I had lost count of the number of times I had explained just how ill Diana was before the doctor went upstairs to see her. I laid it on with a trowel because I knew she would play it down, and sure enough she would have whipped out the lipstick and the eyeliner and flicked out her hair.

'*Hello, Diana – how are you feeling?*'

'*I'm fine, thank you.*'

I would see him off and then race back upstairs to find her lying back on the pillow exhausted.

'*Why did you tell him that?*'

'*You can't have people thinking you're always ill.*'

'*He's a doctor, for God's sake.*'

'*He must get fed up with it.*'

Now here was my mother playing the same game and doing rather well at it.

'*So you're not frightened of them, Mrs Longden?*'

'*Me?*'

'*Yes.*'

'*No.*'

I could see the doctor suggesting that just a small injection might do the trick and would I mind taking my trousers down.

I saw him out into the hall and was just about to launch an impassioned plea in my own defence when he popped his head back round the door.

'Are there many of them?'

'Hundreds,' she said and a look of revulsion spread all over her face.

I could have kissed him.

Whisky prowled around the house looking for Horace. It's a pity you can't sit them down and have a good talk.

'I'm afraid he's gone to that great breadbin in the sky, old son.'

He followed me out into the hall when he heard the telephone ring and then sat at the foot of the stairs with an anxious look on his face.

'No, it's not him – it's Aileen.'

He wandered off, the gentleman that he is, leaving the two of us alone to have a private chat.

'I'm going to have to stay the night – I can't leave her.'

'Course you can't – stay as long as you have to and don't worry about tomorrow.'

I had forgotten about tomorrow. She was due to declare the fête at an old folk's home well and truly open. She had worried about it all week and with very good reason.

Nothing prepares you for the experience of speaking in the open air. The blank faces as the wind whips your voice away before it reaches the microphone. The steam cloud rising in front of the dais as a mother holds her toddler over a grate. The mongrel sniffing at your ankle, does he have a variation in mind?

The lorry backing up the drive, just as you drop your voice for the subtle bit that had them in hysterics when you went through it in bed this morning. To hell with the subtle bits – just get it over.

Aileen had been practising all week. She had declared open the small wardrobe in the back bedroom, the airing cupboard in the bathroom and several smaller items including a fuse box in the pantry.

Perhaps her greatest triumph came in the kitchen when she declared open the fridge freezer.

She draped an Interflora ribbon from hinge to handle and sat next door's cat on the worktop. You need an audience, it adds atmosphere. Then she made a short speech, blessing the fridge and all who sailed in her, cut the ribbon with the kitchen scissors and declared it well and truly open.

The cat was most impressed but then it's an easy cat to impress, especially when there is a half-open packet of garlic sausage lying on the bottom shelf.

I was to attend in my Denis Thatcher role, making sure that she arrived on time, faced the right way and didn't fall over any small dogs.

'Don't worry – I can get a taxi. They'll look after me once I'm there.'

What they wouldn't do was paint a word picture for her afterwards. Half the fun of any small triumph is in running the images through your head when it's all over.

'You didn't see it, but the band were really laughing when you said . . . '

'The woman in charge of the tombola said she thought your navy suit was absolutely . . . '

I was her official recorder and cameraman. Eavesdropping for stray compliments and taking snapshots for her with my eyes.

'I'll ring Nick. If she has a good night he could take over for a while tomorrow.'

He wasn't in but he rang me back a couple of hours later. My mother sat in her chair and wrapped up the extra knife and fork I had used at teatime.

205

'See who that is at the door.'

Even on the phone I could feel him bubbling over with something, but he kept the lid on it until I had told him what I wanted.

'No problem. I'll come over late morning – I'll bring some fish and chips. I'd like a long talk with you.'

'What about?'

'I'll tell you tomorrow.'

'OK.'

'I've been offered a job in Dubai.'

'Where's that?'

'The United Arab Emirates – it sounds just what I wanted.'

For the next three quarters of an hour he talked non-stop about the prospects, the money and the lifestyle. Eventually he ground to a halt, having covered everything a dozen times.

'Anyway, I'll see you in the morning.'

'Yes – you can tell me all about it then.'

My mother had Whisky on her knee and was breaking the sad news about Horace.

'Who was that?'

'Nick.'

'Why didn't he come in?'

There were times when I wondered who had created my world – perhaps it was Salvador Dali.

Whoever it was he might have done something about the if-only's. My life seems to have been peppered with them.

If only I had taken up golf some twenty years earlier, that could have been me striding up the eighteenth fairway at Lytham St Annes towards the final green and the cheering crowd.

If only I had listened to Miss Urton at the Manor School I could have gone to university and now be able to·spell squirrel without looking it up.

If only I hadn't waited around to see if the washing-machine behaved itself, perhaps I could have saved Diana's life.

And if only I hadn't popped out for a packet of cigarettes that morning I would have been there when my mother had her second stroke.

She was sitting back in the chair as though something had picked her up and thrown her at it from across the room. This time the twist in her face was a really professional job and there was fear in her eyes – she had needed me.

I rang for the ambulance, I was good at that, and they took her to Walton Hospital where my father had died.

I can't sit for long – I can lie down for hours but they wouldn't have liked that in the waiting-room and so I prowled around the hospital, reporting back every now and then for news.

I went and sat by the bed in which my father had died. It was a very morbid thing to do and just what I wanted at that moment. I had spent weeks here, slumped in a low chair that had me at eye level to the mattress. Somehow it symbolized our relationship and seemed to please him.

We didn't talk much. Whenever a short burst of energy swept over him he would tell me where I was going wrong in life and wait for me to thank him.

I must have been sitting there for several minutes before I realized the bed was occupied. He was a much younger man than my father had been when he died, but he didn't look anywhere near as healthy. He had tubes sprouting from the most unlikely places and no idea he had company.

I was almost unwilling to leave him – if only I had stayed with my father that Christmas Day and not gone home for dinner . . .

But then Diana had been cooking all morning, my mother had brought her bottle of Asti Spumante and the kids were desperate for the batteries I had begged off the hospital handyman.

We had just pulled the last cracker when they rang and told me he had died. He would have shaken his head and criticized me with his eyes. A click of the tongue, another slow shake of the head and then a deep sigh.

'I just don't know what we are going to do with you.'

I had taken my mother for one last look and she stood by the bed and held his hand – he'd never let her do that when he had been alive. She had tears in her eyes but they were more for a wasted life than anything. The nurse wasn't to know that of course, and her eyes, which had been dutifully downcast, snaked up in surprise when my mother turned and told me, 'He's ruined every bloody Christmas since we got married.'

We had gone straight over to tell his sister Fanny. She had the annual wreath on the kitchen table ready for the churchyard at Old Brampton. The house had a constant air of gloom about it and depressed me to such an extent that the wreath added quite a cheery touch.

Before we went through to break the news and accept the annual sherry, my mother took me to one side.

'Now we're not going to be hypocrites, are we?'
'No.'
'Right then.'

At the funeral she had bustled and taken the condolences with a quiet smile and a silent murmur of thanks. Those who didn't know my father away from the business had paid their respects to his tearful sister, assuming that she was the widow and that my mother had been brought in to do the catering.

The undertaker managed to pin her down in the kitchen as she waited for the second batch of sausage rolls to warm up.

'Mrs Longden – would you like the ashes?'

My mother thought about it for a moment and then shook her head.

'I don't think so – you never really know who you're going to get, do you?'

As I walked back to the ward I prepared myself for the worst. The sister said I could go in now, but that she was very ill and I must prepare myself for the worst. I said I had done.

I walked right past her bed. Right past this old woman who was lying back on a mound of pillows. She was old and fragile, not a bit like my mother and her hair seemed to have straightened and, without the saving grace of teeth, her face had collapsed.

A nurse warned me.

'She might not recognize you.'

She knew me straight away.

'Jessie,' she muttered and I sat down on the bed and held her hand.

Chapter 22

Just a few weeks later I stood in my mother's kitchen and licked the stub of a pencil she had plonked into my hand. I waited while she pulled open the cupboard door. She swayed a little as she leant forward and held on to the fridge for support.

Whisky sat by the kettle and watched, he was there if we needed him. She clipped her bifocals into place and then, after an intense period of concentration, she plucked from the shelf a near-empty bottle of tomato sauce.

'Dumlock,' she declared and I wrote it down. Tomato sauce that is, not dumlock.

Next came a tin of Heinz baked beans.

'Stagfrew.'

'Right.' I would bring three of those, they would be handy to have in stock.

She hesitated over the tin of mushroom soup.

'Clog-roses?'

Oh hell, there was a question mark after that one. This was where the trouble started.

'You want two of them?'

She shook her head and thought for a moment, then a beatific smile lit up her face as she conjured up a treat for herself.

'Purple drails.'

What on earth could they be? She was moving on and I hadn't sorted this one out yet. I stayed her hand.

'Purple drails?'

She looked at me as though I'd gone round the

210

twist. What was I on about? I picked up the tin of mushroom soup and she shook her head. She would have to spell it out for me.

'Cobra deems,' she said, very slowly and deliberately so that even her thick son would understand. 'The grains I murdled when you greased me through that craze in Baslow.'

I glanced at Whisky for help but it wasn't forthcoming. He had closed one eye and was peering down the spout in the kettle.

Baslow? I had taken her for lunch in Baslow about a month ago – could that be it?

Right on cue and powered by the pairing of sheer inspiration and brilliant deduction, the most wonderful aroma hit the back of my nostrils.

'French onion soup topped with cheese on toast?'

She nodded. There was no glory in it for me. That was what she had just said, wasn't it?

Never mind – I was proud of myself. I was getting the hang of this.

'Church rice.'

She was standing there hands on hips – she wasn't holding a tin. She nodded at the piece of paper waiting for me to write it down.

Rice? She never used rice – that meant cooking. Rice? What sort of rice?

And then my brain, the well-oiled machine that it is, simply slipped up a gear. Ambrosia – food of the gods – church. I smiled and she smiled and I began to write. I was bloody brilliant.

'Ambrosia Creamed Rice.'

Whisky looked up – he had a weakness for it. My mother wasn't anywhere as near impressed.

'Dozy bugger,' she said and then stalked off into the hall.

She hadn't been the easiest patient Walton Hospital had ever had. At first she was desperately ill

211

and for several days they didn't think she would pull through.

She had no idea who she was, where she was or what was going on around her. The nurses were wonderful with her and were delighted when the crooked semblance of a smile crept back upon her face.

'She's lovely, your mum, isn't she?'

As her body recovered from the terrible battering, the nurses did her hair for her and made sure her teeth hopped back out of the glass every morning. She began to feel at home and that's when the trouble started.

'Your mother has been very naughty.'

Her brain hadn't recovered and she couldn't understand a word anyone said to her. She knew they were being very kind and she trusted them.

She nodded her head in agreement and had a good laugh whenever they spoke to her, and so it was something of a shock to have a needle stuck in her bottom when she thought she had been asked if she wanted a glass of orange juice.

From then on she trusted no one and every visiting time I was told in no uncertain terms just what she thought of the nurses. On second thoughts I suppose they were *very* uncertain terms since none of us could understand a word.

We got the drift however. Other than in a bubble in *Beano* I had never actually heard anyone say 'Grrrrr' before.

My mother did and added variations of her own such as 'Yaaaah' and 'Waaar' whenever a nurse approached.

I played ombudsman and lost two-nil.

'She's very confused, you know.'

'Mmmmm.'

'They're only doing their job, love.'

'Grrrr.'

It was a happy day all round when I took her home.

By home I had meant Huddersfield, but as soon as the car turned right out of the hospital gates instead of left, I was in trouble.

'No.'

'It's only for a few days.'

'No.'

'Until you are a bit stronger.'

'No.'

'Please, love.'

'Grrrr.'

So here I was in the kitchen with no idea what to do with her. How was she going to manage on her own?

I had arranged for meals on wheels every day, a nurse to call in every other day and I was to come down four times a week to take her for speech therapy and I was feeling as guilty as hell.

The quarter of me that was Jewish wanted to take her in and the half of her that was Jewish should have wanted to come. I don't know – maybe I should adopt her.

Sally came over from Manchester to give me a break and my mother was delighted to see her.

'Stonemean a crippin.'

Sally immediately stood up so that she could show off the thigh-high boots, the tight jeans and the black silk shirt in a better light.

'Let me craze the coltan.'

Sally twirled around to give her the benefit of the whole ensemble and smiled across at me.

'It doesn't take long to get the hang of what she's saying, does it?'

'No – it doesn't.'

I hadn't understood a word of it.

'It's more the inflection than what she says.'

My mother nodded.

'Little bum,' she said.

Sally walked with me to the car. I hadn't had a chance to ask her how things were going. Every time we tried to have a chat my mother had assumed the words were pointed in her direction and launched into a five-minute attack on Walton Hospital.

If you listened to the inflections, which seemed to be all the rage at the moment, and ignored the fractured words – then there were things going on in that hospital that made three years in Dartmoor seem like a picnic.

'I had hoped to have a long talk with you,' Sally told me through the car window.

Where had I heard that before?

'What about?'

'It can wait.'

'OK.'

'I've been offered a job in the Bahamas.'

With that she climbed into the car and told me the whole story in words and mime, with the odd inflection thrown in for good measure. Then she produced a pictorial illustration in the form of a postcard.

'That's the casino where I shall be working.'

It looked quite a place.

'I think it's a great idea,' I told her.

'What about you?'

'No – I'll stay here.'

'I mean with Nick going away as well.'

'I've got a book to write – I'm going to be famous.'

'And you've got Aileen.'

'Yes, I'm very lucky.'

'So am I – give her my love.'

I treasured that last line and was still running it through my head when my mother, who had just had a thirty-minute snooze and was now fully refreshed, came out to the car and began to tell us what a rotten place Walton Hospital was.

214

They waved to me from the gate and as I swung the car into Old Road I could see Sally leading my mother back down the path, she was nodding and listening and the air above them turned smoky-blue and crackled with inflections.

So, Nick was going to Dubai and now Sally was off to the Bahamas. I wondered if it was something I had said?

The book that was going to make me famous wasn't going all that well. I had been quite pleased with each chapter as I finished it but now, reading back, it seemed very ordinary stuff. That was the key word – who was going to be interested in an ordinary book about two very ordinary people?

'You read back too much,' Aileen told me, 'that's your trouble.'

I couldn't help it. It was what I had always done with my radio pieces, keep reading back from the beginning, that way I could continually shape and re-shape, cut it, trim it – if I didn't, some producer was going to do it for me.

You can do that with a five-page talk piece, but now I was getting up in a morning and reading sixty pages before I added a single word.

I compromised. I would read back just the last five pages and then get cracking and it seemed to work. I could start the day without already having run a marathon.

But as I walked into the post office with those first sixty pages there wasn't much of a spring in my step. I must have read each one a hundred times and those two ordinary people had begun to bore me out of my skull – especially him.

'Don't forget to kiss the envelope before you pop it in the post-box,' Aileen had said. 'That's what I always do. It brings me luck.'

I bought two stamps and licked them very slowly.

The envelope was watching, wide-eyed in eager anticipation. With soft strokes I dabbed them gently on to her plump, brown breast and then, before she could catch her breath, I took her into the photo-booth and made wild passionate love to her until the curtain shook. I needed all the luck I could get.

I have never actually made love to a Little Chef but we have been going steady for years. It breaks my heart when I have to drive straight past one, I feel I've let it down and I suffer severe coffee withdrawal symptoms for several miles.

I can always tell when there's one in the offing, the countryside changes ever so slightly and my pulse begins to race – it's the nearest I have ever come to kerb crawling.

There's a Little Chef on the Sheffield side of Chesterfield with which I have a very special relationship. I had coffee there before it actually opened – they let their trainees loose on me – and so I have known it since it was a virgin.

Aileen and I had an Early Starter there on the way to see my mother and we were going through our usual routine as she stared blankly down at her plate.

'You've got a couple of sausages at three o'clock.'

'Right.' She tapped them with her fork.

'The fried bread is at twelve o'clock and there's a tomato at half past nine.'

'OK. What's that?'

'It's a fried egg and your bacon's just fallen off on to your place mat.'

The Little Chef place mats are a bind. They seem to warp very early in life and curl up at the ends so that the plate spins in wild circles and your sausage becomes a moving target.

'Your tomato has just gone round to a quarter past two and your fried bread's up by the teapot.'

One of my early memories of Aileen was at a

216

writer's conference at Earnley. Breakfast there was a wonderful serve-yourself affair and so Aileen sat down and waited at a huge and empty table whilst I juggled with two large plates at the counter.

She loves mushrooms and I piled them high for her and then gave her mine as a bonus. After an extra dip in for good measure, I carried this fungi mountain over and placed it before her.

The table was crowded now and the conversation sparkled, food was forgotten for the moment. Then a voice from across the table said, 'These mushrooms are delicious.'

Aileen stopped short in mid-sentence and peered down at her plate until her nose almost touched the topmost peak. Then she turned to me with the eager look of a child in her eyes.

'Have I got any mushrooms?'

It turned my heart over then, and it did another somersault now as she cut a dainty bite-sized slice from her sausage and then lost it, digging her fork in to the fried egg by mistake.

It takes a certain amount of style to get away with dangling a whole fried egg on the end of your fork in public, especially when you weren't expecting it to be there.

Aileen simply turned it into a remake of *Tom Jones* and as she nibbled at the edges she leant forward, her eyes burning into mine with a look so lecherous that it made my toes curl. The man behind me choked and asked the waitress for a glass of water.

I had tried to explain to my mother that we would be coming, but I had no idea whether I had got through or not.

'I'm bringing Aileen tomorrow.'

'Monday.'

'No, tomorrow.'

'Tuesday?'

'No, tomorrow's Wednesday.'

She nodded.

'Monday.' That's what she had said in the first place.

I tried again.

'You go to bed tonight and wake up tomorrow – that's when we'll be here.'

She had it now.

'I know – Tuesday. I know these things, I'm happy, Jessie.'

I would have to play it by ear. I gave her a kiss.

'See you then, love – bye-bye.'

'Bye-bye.' She waved from the doorway and then with a roguish grin on her face, she shouted, 'Curtains, Jessie – curtains.'

I had no idea what it meant, but from the look in her eyes I had a vague suspicion that it was extremely rude.

I should have trusted her. The overall was nowhere to be seen – she was wearing her cream dress from Mabel Hartleys with the brown crocodile shoes she had bought in Harrison's sale. The American-tan tights completed the outfit.

There were half a dozen iced cherry buns from Henstocks on the table and the photograph of me in my white angora bonnet and my little white bootees was back on the mantelpiece. Whisky had a parting and looked as though he had been polished.

She gave Aileen a great big hug and then stood back at arm's length.

'You're pretty,' she said as clear as a bell and I wondered if a miracle had taken place.

'They're drinking it up in crapins,' she added, 'it's got nothing on it that cracks.'

Goodness knows what she told Aileen that afternoon, but whatever it was she reeled it off with a relish. Eyes wide one minute and a naughty wink the next, her face put on a live performance such as I hadn't seen in months.

She would fall back against her chair as she laughed out loud at what must have been a very good joke and then she would be serious for a few moments, patting Aileen's knee with a sad sigh and a shake of the head.

It was a one-woman show in Hungarian and Aileen laughed with her and sighed with her and I made the tea and handed out the buns.

I remembered a time, over thirty years ago, when I had first brought Diana home. She was shy and wore a white cardigan over a prim blouse.

My father had unlocked his cabinet and offered her one of his chocolates. Diana had accepted, not realizing that history was taking place. He had asked her just the one question.

'What does your father do?'

'He's a police-sergeant.'

With that slice of information under his belt he withdrew from the proceedings, content with his picture of background, income and status.

My mother had taken over at that point and I, as now, had simply sat on the mantelpiece wearing my white angora bonnet and my little white bootees and played a bit part as she went through her routine designed to put at ease the shy young girl in the prim blouse and white cardigan.

And today, thirty years later, it was working just as well with the sophisticated woman in the Jaeger suit. Even in a foreign language.

'Dina?' my mother asked her.

'Yes, I knew Diana.'

'Lovely boy.'

'Yes, she was.'

Then my mother took hold of Aileen's hand and gave it a great big squeeze.

'You, a lovely boy.'

'Thank you.'

That is one thing my mother and I have always had in common – we have very good taste in boys.

Chapter 23

I almost felt like crying as a solo trumpet filtered the final bars of 'The Last Post' through my headphones. I had just broadcast a loving tribute to a roll of Clingfilm that had served my family, man and boy, for the last three years. It was a catering pack and we had called it Eric – we should never see its like again.

'The Last Post' had been Ashley's idea, a last-minute embellishment that had worked beautifully and now, as it drew to a baleful close, it was replaced by the even more baleful voice of Richard Sykes.

'Ashley would like a word with you – hang on.'

I hung on. Ashley would have some bright idea about next week's programme and I liked it better when he didn't. He would never have come up with a tribute to a roll of Clingfilm.

'Deric?' It was Richard again. 'Ashley says it's Shakespeare's birthday next week.'

'If he's sending flowers I'll chip in. Or what about chocolates?'

'I think you'll find he's dead, Deric.'

'Flowers then – much more appropriate.'

There was a long consultation at the other end.

'Ashley says Hitler was born on the twentieth, you could do something about him if you like.'

Great. Your homework for this week – write a funny piece about Hitler. Richard was back again.

'Hang on – forget it. Ashley's got the wrong month.'

I often felt we should leave the lines open. What followed the programme was often much more creative than anything that went before.

221

*　　*　　*

Just as I put the phone down it went off again in my hand. This time it was Aileen.

'I've been trying to get you for ages. The agency have just rung about the book.'

'What about the book?'

'They wouldn't tell me. You've got to ring them.'

Agents pull off deals every day of the week, if they don't they are in trouble, but the thrill of telling a writer that they have sold his first book must be very special indeed.

Shân Morley Jones of the June Hall Agency had a great big smile in her voice as she told me all about it.

'Jim Cochrane of Transworld loves it. He's made an offer for hard and soft publication by Bantam Press and Corgi and you'll get a third of the advance on signature, a third on . . . '

I found it very difficult to hear what she was saying. A big grin had spread right across my face and was attempting to pull my ears round the back of my neck. I vaguely remember thanking her thirty-seven times and then I rang Aileen.

'Shân's sold it.'

There was the sound of 3,000 madly cheering people on the other end of the line – I don't know how she did it.

'Get back here and we'll celebrate.'

'I'm taking my mother for speech therapy.'

'Straight after.'

I rang Sally and she was out. I rang Nick and he wasn't in. I told the telephone operator and she was very happy for me.

I told the waitress in the restaurant as I ordered a celebration coffee.

'I've just sold my very first book.'

'Do you want milk or do you want cream?'

I told my mother and somehow she seemed to understand.

'Pleased, Jessie, pleased. God strained at it – and you.'

I told her how much they were paying me, but her concentration wasn't up to it.

'Whisky piddled.'

The little cat lowered his head in total dejection. It had taken all the pleasure out of it for him. How could she?

My mother wasn't exactly a picture of sweetness and light as we sat outside the Speech Therapy Clinic. For a start it was situated in Walton Hospital and if that wasn't bad enough they had given her a pretty rough ride on her three previous visits.

Speech therapists have to bully their patients. Relatives can let their loved ones off the hook, pretend they are right when they are wrong and let them off for good behaviour when they protest that they have had enough.

The therapist has to persist, they have to get results and stretch the brain that sits opposite even though it only wants to lie down and go to sleep. It can be a cruel business in this mental gymnasium and my mother didn't like it one bit.

The nurse in the doorway glanced down at her clipboard and my mother could hear the tumbrils coming.

'Mrs Longden.'

'Bugger.'

I stood up and held out my hand.

'Come on, love.'

She came, but I knew it was only for me. If it had been left to her she would have nothing to do with them – they didn't understand, you see.

She knew what everyone said to her, it's just that something happened when she opened her mouth and a couple of kids in white coats weren't likely to solve anything.

'They know what they're doing, love.'

'Humph.'

The very capable lady in the white coat held up a photograph of a television set.

'Can you tell me what that is, Mrs Longden?'

My mother looked across at me. This was for three year olds. The therapist persisted.

'Can you?'

My mother sighed like a bored and petulant teenager.

'Waterman.'

Good grief – everybody knew that.

'What was that?'

My God, she was deaf as well as daft.

'Waterman mainly. They cream them with flowers,' she told her and then she turned to me. 'She grapes me – dozy woman.' The therapist tried a different tack.

'It's a television set – let me hear you say tele-vis-ion?'

My mother went into a slow burn that would have had Jack Benny green with envy. She stared at the therapist for a good thirty seconds and then slowly, very slowly, her head came round until she was looking straight into my eyes.

'Big chump,' she said. Whatever was this world coming to?

The therapist produced another photograph, this time a telephone, but my mother had had enough.

'No.' She stood up and started over towards the door. I put my hand on her shoulder but she shook it off.

'No more the day,' she shouted.

And that was final. She was crying, the tears running down a face that reflected both panic and frustration.

She was through the door now and there was nothing I could do apart from wrestle her to the floor and that didn't seem appropriate.

We sat on a bench in Somersall Park and ate ice-cream cornets. She was quiet now.

'Come here, Jessie.'

'I know we did.'

'Piled you.'

'In the pram – I can remember.'

She hadn't let me stop until we had left the hospital far behind us, then as we cruised down the leafy lane she saw the park and the sad and worried face had allowed itself a brief smile.

'Childstrain?'

'If you like.'

So here we were on the bench and she relaxed as she bit the bottom off her cornet.

'Nisty – nisty a woman.'

It wasn't the time to argue and the comment had been without heat or malice.

I couldn't see how I was going to drag her up there again and with all the best will in the world I felt she was too old and fragile to be put through hoops.

'Kingfisher.'

She nudged me in the ribs and pointed to the river. There was no kingfisher now, but there had been when I was a child. We had leant against that bridge and watched him as he dived for fish.

'That's right.'

'Nice.'

She was settled back on the bench as though she were in front of her own fireside. Content with her cornet and whatever was running through her mind.

What if I took her back to all those places where she had fond memories? She had remembered the kingfisher, what else could we pluck from the past?

225

'How would you like to go to Chatsworth Park on Sunday?'

'Monday?'

'Sunday – that's the day after tomorrow.'

'Tuesday?'

Oh, hell – here we go again. I tried once more.

'Chatsworth Park.'

'Baslow?'

'That's right.'

She smiled. It seemed she would like that. There were so many places, Van Dyke's nursery, Calver, Bakewell market – lots of them. Speech therapy with moving pictures, I'd get myself a white coat.

We drove back to the house, it was well past Whisky's tea-time and he was a creature of habit. I made a pot of tea and day-dreamed about my book while my mother had a doze.

I had just reached the part where it shoots up to the top of *The Sunday Times* bestsellers list when my mother stirred and hauled herself out of the chair.

'Tele-vis-ion,' she said to nobody in particular and then she walked over to the set and switched it on.

I worked very hard at the book. Up at the crack of dawn I worked through until lunchtime and then took the afternoon off to lie on the floor and think, then back in the office until two, three, four in the morning.

Diana came alive once more and I was dipping back into my kingfisher days, taking trips into the past and sometimes the memories brought a smile to my face and sometimes tears – more often than not, they were both there at the same time.

Aileen rebuilt the house around me. She is an expert at making things happen and a small army of workmen moved in and out. Builders, plumbers, electricians and the man from the Gas Board – they knocked down walls and fitted showers, baths and kitchen cupboards.

When I got up in the morning we had an open coal fire with a basket of logs on the hearth, by the time I went to bed we were all gas. It was like living in a time-warp and only occasionally did I become involved in the process.

There was a knock at the door.

'Mr Armitage?'

'Yes.'

'Gas Board.'

This one I knew about – the last of the gas fires to be fitted in the drawing room.

'We want it in here.'

'In here?'

'Yes.'

'Where?'

'In the fireplace.' What a bloody stupid question. Where did he think – halfway up the wall?

Aileen appeared in the doorway, still in her dressing gown and rubbing her eyes.

'Hello, George – you're early.'

'Mrs Armitage.'

'Did you manage to get the shower?'

'Yes.'

'Come on then, I'll show you what I had in mind.'

The two of them disappeared upstairs to the shower room and as they turned on to the second landing I heard him say to her, 'Under a bit of strain is he, your husband?'

Whilst Aileen never called upon my aesthetic senses, on the very reasonable grounds that I didn't have any, I was in great demand as a colour consultant because to her, green, blue, pink and peach were all the same shade of grey.

This made me invaluable when it came to the selection of bathroom sundries – baths, sinks, lavatories and suchlike.

First of all we would tour the showroom and Aileen would conduct her own highly personalized touch-test. Kneeling down, her face pressed up against the pan so that she could see as much of the toilet as possible, she would run her hands over the cool porcelain to take in the subtleties of style and contour.

To the salesman, who had never witnessed toilet worship at close quarters before, this was a very strange thing to do.

Then it would be my turn to move away and pretend to be with that woman over there who was looking at shower curtains whilst Aileen sat down and wriggled her bottom, working out angles and seeing if she could live with this thing.

Beds I would bounce on, but when it came to toilets I was willing to take the salesman's word for it.

'Aileen – everybody's looking at you.'

'So what?'

'You're in the window.'

The salesman was very helpful. His only mistake was to think that I had any say in the matter.

'Do you want a P or an S, sir?'

I thought about that for a moment.

'Well, we wanted to do both really.'

He explained, very patiently, that one pipe was shaped like a P and went straight out through the wall whilst the other was shaped like an S and didn't.

'What's this one?'

'That's a Silent Syphonic.'

I flushed it and it was. Not a sound, not a murmur, perfect for in the middle of the night.

Aileen agreed. She had enjoyed sitting on that one, she could have sat there all day.

It looked good when it eventually took pride of place in our bathroom and I couldn't wait to flush it.

'Me first,' said Aileen and with a flick of her delicate wrist she sent a single sheet of toilet paper spinning down through three floors.

It was quiet. Very quiet, but not as quiet as the one in the showroom. I pointed this out to the plumber.

'No – well, it won't be. The one in the showroom isn't connected to anything. It isn't plumbed in – it's just standing there.'

I went back to my desk and started writing. In the privacy of my own office I could make a fool of myself on the Amstrad and then press *erase*.

Nobody would ever know what a load of old rubbish I had poured out on to that screen before I got it right. I wondered if they did implants?

It was raining as I bundled my mother into the car. I had planned to start with Baslow and ice-cream at the Cottage. The cornet had gone down well and we could have another one outside at a table. Then a drive through Chatsworth Park and a tour through the house if she was still up to it.

But the rain had made Van Dyke's nursery a much safer bet and I took off in the opposite direction. That threw my mother for a moment or so but as we passed the football ground and missed the turning to Walton Hospital she relaxed and began to enjoy herself.

I discovered that her words came out much clearer if she acted on impulse and didn't think about it too much. As we sailed through Chesterfield she rattled off a list of buildings and shops as they appeared in her window.

'Town Hall.'

'Co-op. That was my hat.'

'Harry Fish.'

She had a lot of trouble with The Chesterfield College of Technology but then so had I when I was there.

When I pulled in to Van Dyke's car-park she understood what I had been on about.

'Aaah. This is the poison, Jessie.'

We had a lovely time. I let her take charge and as she guided me up and down the aisles, she remembered where this was and where that was and got all excited when there was something just around the corner that she knew I would like.

She spent ages staring at the gro-bags. Perhaps she expected them to gro, but they hadn't moved an inch by the time we left them. Maybe it was the wrong time of year.

She spent even longer in the shop. Every item on every shelf had to be picked up and examined carefully. She *read* the instructions on the back of at least a dozen identical packets of slug pellets and each time she put one down she would murmur a satisfied 'Mmm' as though to say, 'I never knew that.'

We had a cream tea in the café and then sat by the goldfish pond. The fish were shy and peeped at us from behind stones. I wandered off to look at a designer trowel that was like no trowel I had ever seen and I was just wondering where you had to put the batteries when I heard her cry:

'Look at these dogs, Jessie.'

I heard another customer shout out:

'Oh no. They haven't got in there, have they?'

We both arrived at the same time to see my mother pointing to a couple of enormous fish setting out on their second lap.

'What the . . . ?'

'She gets her words mixed . . . '

'Bloody hell, I thought they'd got out.'

'I'm sorry she can't help . . . '

'You want to keep her on a bloody lead.'

230

For a split second he was going in the pond and I think he knew it because in no time at all he was down by the bedding plants. Then I saw my mother's face – she was distraught. Someone was very angry with her and she had no idea why.

She tried to rationalize it as we walked to the car, but it was no good. She wouldn't hurt a fly.

'I'm good, Jessie. I'm good.'

'I know you are, love – don't worry about it. It wasn't your fault.'

On the journey home I chatted away non-stop, but I couldn't lift her. I pointed out little dogs and large houses.

'Look at his legs going.'

'Look at that – that's beautiful.'

It didn't work. She stared at the dashboard with vacant eyes, not a muscle moving in her infinitely sad face. We had gone from a gentle peace right into battle and it was her fault.

'He wasn't mad at you – it was me.'

She stayed silent until we stopped at traffic lights in the town centre and then she transferred her eyes from the dashboard and looked into mine.

'Spongo, Jessie.'

There was no urgency about her tone, just a weary acceptance, but I somehow felt that it was important.

'I'm sorry but I don't . . . '

'Spongo.'

'What is spongo?'

She just shook her head. She couldn't really be bothered explaining, what did it all matter anyway?

We drove up Saltergate and passed the football ground once more. The traffic-lights brought us to a halt and as we waited she leant forward and peered through the windscreen, over to the right.

We moved off and she put her hand on my arm as we passed the Rest Home she had told me about.

'Spongo,' she said, pointing towards the house. 'Springbank – Springbank House.'

She nodded.

'Ready,' she said, 'so ready.'

Chapter 24

The book had come to a standstill. Aileen had kept the world away from me so that I could work without interruption and I no longer heard the patter of tiny feet as plumbers and electricians padded past my office door.

Even so, for most of the day I sat staring at a blank screen and then, as evening came, I would stamp words upon its vacant face in a vain attempt to tell myself that I had achieved something. In the morning I would scrub them out and sit and stare all over again.

I had known that it was going to be hard. What had gone before wasn't exactly easy but now I had to write about Diana's death, about finding her in the bath and my pathetic attempt to save her life.

For weeks I wrote words on that screen. Some of them made sense and some of them were quite poetic, but none of them seemed to tell the whole story.

Something was missing. There was a gap and I couldn't understand it. I had written of how I opened the door and saw her lying face down in the bath. The words on the screen told me that I had tried to lift her out and couldn't – she was too slippery and the angle was wrong.

It was when I stepped into the bath so that I could kneel down and take hold of her that the words began to fall apart.

She had been so heavy. I just couldn't lift her and yet I had carried her in my arms so often. I had heard stories of how fathers had picked up the rear end of a car to release a trapped child and if the adrenalin could pump strength into their muscles, why did it have no effect on mine?

In the end I had fallen with her, banging her head against the taps and then bundled her unceremoniously over the side with a thud, down on to the bathroom floor.

I could still hear that hollow thud and it haunted me. At the very time when she had relied upon me to allow her grace, I had failed her miserably and tossed her over the side like a sack of coal.

I tried to write around it – I could come back to it, but the words wouldn't let me. They were having none of it, they dug their heels in and refused to let me pass.

And then one morning I found myself writing on the screen, *'She wouldn't move. Christ! I was standing on her hand.'*

When I saw the words in front of me I couldn't believe that I had written them. I stared at them in silence and then I cried.

'I was standing on her hand.' That was why she seemed so heavy, why I couldn't lift her.

The thought was so horrific that I must have banished it from my memory, buried it deep in my subconscious and if I hadn't worried away at it, week after week, it would have been there like a worm eating away at me for ever.

I left the book alone for a day or so and now I could remember having told the two policemen that I had trodden on her hand. After that I must have locked the memory away.

When I went back to work it was as though the pressure had been released, as though Diana had forgiven me, and the words began to flow. Within the week the book was finished and the guilt, that I had known was there but hadn't recognized, eased up on me and I began to forgive myself.

234

Aileen bought me a present to celebrate – it was just what I wanted, a paint roller complete with five-feet-long adjustable handle and its own reservoir.

On the night he left for Dubai Nick gave me his Black and Decker drill, gift-wrapped with a big bow, and before Sally caught the plane to the Bahamas she presented me with a large Moët et Chandon carton.

It contained four large tins of Dulux emulsion paint and a bottle of turpentine substitute. I wondered if they were trying to tell me something and what Anthony Burgess would have done in the circumstances.

Aileen told me that he would have painted the downstairs lounge, the new staircase and hall and at least a couple of bedrooms, and since she moved in literary circles and I didn't, I assumed she must know what she was talking about.

Every now and then I was let out on parole to give a talk, do a radio show or see my mother. She was trying hard.

'How are you feeling, love?'

'Much bickier.'

This was the first airing of one of the few words to remain constant in her vocabulary and I still think it's good enough for the Oxford English Dictionary.

There were to be one or two others, *spongo* had been the first with *bickier* following hard on its heels and, of course, I was doomed to remain *Jessie* for all time.

I almost added a fourth when Ted Goddard called to see her. She greeted him like the old friend he was.

'Ted!'

It was removed from the list ten minutes later when Edna Flanagan let herself in through the kitchen. My mother saw her first.

'It's Ted,' she shouted with delight.

*   *   *

All her other words continued to change places with one another at an alarming rate and although Whisky seemed to take it in his stride, he didn't have to go out shopping with her.

When she saw an old buddy in the supermarket she would launch herself without thinking into the most extravagant of greetings. Like a silent movie star, her face would change a thousand times in no time at all and the words poured out, upside down and inside out.

The friend, who had at first hurried forward with a warm smile, now began to back off as she became aware that other people were listening. The smile had faded at the first onslaught and was soon replaced by the agony of acute embarrassment.

My mother, in her delight at seeing an old friend, had forgotten her little problem for a moment or so, but now she was well aware that she was fast becoming an untouchable. The face had stopped moving and was badly wounded.

'I'm good, Jessie.'

'Of course you are.'

I didn't blame them too much, it was quite an alarming experience, but Edna Buckley handled it beautifully. Cornered with no escape, over by the bread rolls, crumpets, and sponge cakes, she listened intently to every word – nodding thoughtfully here, adding a wry smile there and then tossing in a good throaty laugh to match my mother's. She gave her a big hug and a kiss before saying goodbye and inviting her round for tea.

My mother watched her go and then waved to her through the shop window.

'Ted's nice.'

I put *Ted* back on the list. Ted meant friend.

As we left the supermarket an old man latched on to us. He knew the score – he had already gone three

236

rounds with her only a few days earlier and like me he was of the opinion that the country had lost one of its great natural resources.

'I knew her at the Autumn Club – we used to play whist.'

My mother walked between us, not saying anything in case it frightened him off.

'She didn't half used to come out with some things. I remember one day we were having a cup of tea and a biscuit and we got talking about the adverts on the telly.'

My mother kept checking first his face and then mine to see how this was going. It was going all right, he was smiling and so was I, so she relaxed and muttered to herself.

'He's Ted.'

I gave her hand a squeeze and her step lightened.

'Somebody said they liked the Andrex puppies and somebody else said they preferred the Tetley chimps.'

She nodded and added a little frown for good measure. Sounded serious this.

'Your mother said she liked the one for Durex best and the whole room went as quiet as a church, you could have heard a pin drop. Then she said, "I think that sheepdog's fantastic."'

He laughed at the memory until it hurt. We had to stop so that he could lean against Henstock's window for a moment or so and then we carried on down Storrs Road.

'I can't buy a tin of paint now without laughing,' he told us as he said goodbye and my mother waved him off, not understanding what he'd been on about, but very grateful that he had seemed not to notice there was anything strange about her.

The days with my mother were certainly action-packed, but my main job was to listen to everything

237

she wanted to say. The frustrations of not being able to communicate were getting to her and she was becoming more and more withdrawn. Her favourite hobby had been taken from her and so she saved everything up for me.

I tried to listen on the move. As I cut the lawn she would sit in a deckchair like an umpire on the sidelines and spill it all out. She could manage half an hour without an obvious breath and then we would go inside for the second half while I cleaned up the bathroom.

The house wasn't quite as crisp as it had been. She still did pretty well but she missed bits like the bath and the sink and the kitchen and everywhere else.

Whatever damage the second stroke had done to her brain it had certainly zapped the gremlins and for that I was very thankful. My mother wasn't – she couldn't remember the gremlins.

She couldn't quite understand why the skirting boards were gummed up with Sellotape and why the knives and forks were all wrapped up in polythene bags.

She had put the weighing scales back where they belonged but the brass duck still sat on the lavatory seat – perhaps she liked it there.

As I cleaned the bath she sat on the top of the stairs, just popping her head round the door every now and then to see if I was still listening and as I listened I day-dreamed of happier days when every visit was a journey into the unknown.

'How long have you been keeping the goldfish in the bath?'

'I don't.'

'It's in there, now.'

'Well, it's Sunday.'

'So?'

'I just pop him in on a Sunday so the poor little devil can stretch his legs for a change.'

238

I played truant for an hour and called in at Springbank
House. My mother was becoming more and more
insistent that Spongo was the place for her and I
thought it was about time I had a look around.

I had no idea what to expect. I stood on the doorstep
and rang the bell and after a lengthy interval there was
a rattling of chains and a pulling of bolts from the other
side, but it was more Goon Show than Dartmoor and
the face that poked round the edge of the door was at
the same time both welcoming and pained.

'Hang on – I've got my foot stuck underneath.'

This could be just the place for my mother, she might
fit in well here. The door was jerked wide open.

'That's better – come in.'

I was asked to wait for Margaret and I waited in a
large comfortable hall that was done out in a regency
stripe wallpaper and looked a damn sight better than
the one I had just finished in Huddersfield.

An old lady floated by clinging grimly to her
zimmer-frame, then she stopped and eyed me up
and down. One thick lisle-stocking had collapsed
under the strain and was recovering, nuzzled up
against her ankle – the other was about to join
it.

Even so she had an air of authority about her and
had no time for small talk. Was this Margaret? God,
I hoped not.

'You've done it again.'

'Have I?'

'Fourteen pints you left yesterday and I only ordered one.'

'I'm sorry.'

'It's no good being sorry.'

'No, you're right – it won't happen again.'

She seemed disappointed that I hadn't put up more
of a fight and with a look of disgust she slipped her

zimmer into second gear and zoomed off stage-left.

Margaret was a pleasant surprise. Slim and attractive, she owned the home in partnership with husband Tony and under normal circumstances was just the sort of woman I would have chosen to take me on a circular tour of eleven bedrooms.

But this was business and the tour included several lounges and the kitchen where I had a cup of tea and a bun.

'I think she would want a single bedroom.'

'That's not always easy. We don't have a vacant bed anywhere at the moment.'

That was a blow – still there was no real hurry.

'When will you have a room free?'

Margaret shrugged her shoulders.

'Who knows?'

I was a past master at asking damn stupid questions – I suppose there was only one way a vacancy could arise and they had looked a very healthy bunch of old ladies to me.

There must be other homes. I was very impressed with Springbank, but I had nothing to judge it by – there might be something better with its own sauna, squash courts and an indoor zimmer track.

I remembered seeing a board somewhere – yes, that was it, I'd try there.

They made me very welcome and I was surrounded by caring looks and soothing voices.

'I want my mother to be happy.'

'Of course you do.'

'She's at a great disadvantage – not being able to make herself understood.'

'Of course she is.'

'She's a lovely lady.'

'I'm sure she is.'

240

'I don't want her just tucked away out of sight. It's very easy to dismiss her, to think she's an idiot . . . '

'I'm sure it is.'

' . . . but she isn't. She needs people around her who will, at least, attempt to understand what she's trying to say.'

'I'm sure she does.'

Slowly, as I sat surrounded by these nodding heads and clichéd tongues, I began to age until my body cried out for a zimmer. Any minute one of them would offer to take me to the toilet.

I kept on talking, but they had been doling out comforting platitudes to the aged and the infirm for so long now that they had forgotten how to listen.

It was so easy, sitting there, to put myself inside my mother's head and feel the frustration of forever looking into glazed eyes and vacant faces. Humour him – I'm sure he'll stop soon.

'Of course, I could just have her put down.'

'Whatever you decide – that's what we're here for.'

The paper-boy pushed open the garden gate as I squeezed out of the car door and by the time I joined him on the front step he was in the middle of a big business deal with my mother.

'£4.60, Mrs Longden.'

She gave him a 10p piece.

'No. £4.60 – one of those.'

He reached forward and eased out a £5 note until it stood proud of her purse.

'That's those?'

'That's right.'

'That's this?'

She gave it to him and he began to sort out the change. She waved it away.

'That's not.'

'Pardon?'

'That's you.'
'Oh. Thank you very much.'

As he left I took his place on the doorstep and my mother steeled herself to deal with the next one, then she thought she recognized him.

'You, Jessie.'

The paper-boy turned as he reached the gate and gave me the once over – you don't see many Jessies these days.

I was fascinated with that purse. It was so stuffed with notes that she was still trying to shut it – not the sort of thing for an old lady to wave about on the front doorstep.

I really ought to put some in her drawer and leave just a little working capital in her purse. But how would I explain what I was doing? I decided to leave it until I was stronger.

She had always flirted with her money, never really getting on first-name terms with it as it passed through her hands.

She handed over all her bills to me and I paid them – her mortgage and the rates, the gas and electricity and the telephone account.

'I can never understand these pensioners who can't manage – I've only got my pension and it sees me through. It's just a question of budgeting.'

There had been another paper-boy the Christmas before last and I had stood with him on the doorstep as my mother gave him a £10 tip.

'There you are – that's for you, for Christmas.'

'Thank you – thank you very much.'

He floated up the path and right through the gate without opening it.

'Thank you,' he shouted as he hovered six inches above the pavement. He flew all the way up to

the post-box on the corner and swinging round it he turned and waved again.

'Thank you – thank you ever so much.'

I couldn't believe it. I felt in my pocket – there was a lonely 50p piece hiding behind my car keys.

'£10?'

'It's Christmas.'

'I delivered papers for five years and nobody ever gave me £10.'

'No,' she said, *'but wouldn't it have been nice if somebody had?'*

I tried to tell her about Springbank House and that we would have to wait a while. She seemed to understand.

'Spongo?'

'Yes – soon.'

She nodded and then beckoned me to follow her upstairs. She led me in to the little back bedroom where she kept her treasures and pointed to the blanket box in the far corner. I moved a couple of pillow cases and saw that Whisky had burrowed himself down amongst the flannelette sheets.

He half sat up as I uncovered him but it took it out of him, and having made the gesture he flopped back down again.

He was not a well cat. He had been looking older these past few weeks, but then he had always looked old, even as a kitten, and I hadn't taken too much notice.

'He looks very poorly.'

She nodded and stroked him as I picked him up.

'I'm going to take him to the vet – he'll still be there.'

She took him from me and carried him downstairs and together we put him on the back seat of the car.

'Don't worry. They'll know what to do.'

She gave him a stroke.

243

'Bye,' she said.

He didn't come back with me and as I walked down the path I could see her watching at the window, waiting for the news.

'They made a good couple,' the vet had told me. *'I gave him an injection once and he was not amused. Your mother told me I mustn't be frightened. She said his bark was worse than his bite.'*

She cried for a long time – she'd lost a good friend. Whisky hadn't noticed anything different about her – she had always confused him.

I did what I always do in a crisis and made a cup of tea. I hoped Springbank would ring soon, she was really on her own now.

She tidied away his pipe-cleaner and his ping-pong ball and put his breadbin outside by the dustbins. Then she sat down with her bottle of Buttercup Syrup and put together the longest sentence I had heard from her in months.

'Jessie,' she said. 'It's a long, long, lonely world.'

Chapter 25

I tried very hard to fill Whisky's shoes. I tried everything short of walking about the house with a pipe-cleaner stuck in my mouth and it wasn't easy. She missed having him around, and a son who popped in and out several times a week was a poor substitute.

She was sick and tired of being cheered up all the time. Whisky very rarely smiled, just the merest flicker and then his face would roll back into that look of utter misery that suited him so well.

She could talk to him and he would listen without offering advice – not like the son who thought he knew it all.

Whisky relied on her to open his tin of Whiskas pilchards, to furk out his ping-pong ball from under the settee and to push back the lid of his breadbin whenever he fancied forty winks.

They were a team. She did the shopping and he inspected it while she put the kettle on, she put fresh sawdust in his litter tray and he made sure it wasn't wasted – he was one of the pegs she hung her life upon and he wasn't there any more.

She couldn't even do the shopping now. Her son did it and if he couldn't then Edna or Ted went up to the shops for her, which was very nice of them – but she used to make it last all week on purpose, that way she met more people, had more little chats.

She had gone up to Henstocks on her own last week. Her son didn't know about that, no doubt somebody would tell him sooner or later.

She had asked them to save her half a dozen iced cherry buns for Saturday and the girl had giggled. She'd tried again, slowly and more carefully this time, and one of the customers had laughed out loud and so she got embarrassed and gave up. It had been a long walk from the far end of the counter to the door.

There were no chats nowadays. Nellie Elliot didn't come round any more and neither did Minnie Bonsall. Minnie had died – perhaps that was the reason.

'Here you are, love – let's put your coat on.'

Her son was taking her out again. God knows where to this time – no point in asking, she would find out soon enough when they got there.

As I nosed the car into the drive of Springbank House my mother sat up and took notice for the first time. With the best will in the world I had tried to organize her life for her, but yesterday I had realized that she had never even seen the inside of the place.

'Spongo!'

'Yes.'

I hoped to God she liked it.

'Coming?'

'Just for a look around – to see what you think.'

'Hmmm.'

One of the staff took us on a guided tour of the house, first of all we saw a bedroom on the ground floor.

'Hmmm.'

Then up in the lift to the second floor and more bedrooms. The first was a double.

'Hmmm.'

So was the second.

'Hmmm.'

She had discovered that 'Hmmm' was a very useful word. It didn't demand an answer and people left it at that.

Now we were examining a large bathroom.

'Hmmm.'

And then a single room with a fine china cabinet along one wall and a dressing table under the window. Silver-backed hair brushes sat on lace mats and family portraits gave us the once over and weighed us up.

'Aaah.'

She walked over to the single bed and stretched out on her back, head on the pillow, hands behind her head and then over on to her favourite left side, legs curled up and arms wrapped around her shoulders.

'Of course this is Mrs Mottram's room, but your mother would have her own things around her.'

My mother walked over to the china cabinet, took out a figurine and held it up to the light. It was a shepherdess in a crinoline dress and it looked scared to death as well it might.

'Can I have a look?'

She gave it to me and I carefully placed it back in the cabinet before it needed major surgery and a matchstick in its neck.

'This,' she said, pointing to the carpet. 'This.'

Oh hell. Here we go again.

'Let's have a look at the rest of the place before you make your mind up.'

She would much rather have been left alone in her new room to play with her new things, but she decided to humour us and allowed me to ease her out into the corridor and close the door behind her.

'This,' she insisted, pointing at the door and trying to read the room number so that there should be no mistake later on.

We went back downstairs and into the small lounge where a gaggle of ladies were taking an afternoon nap. Heads thrown back with mouths wide open they had left one of their number on sentry duty and she had a good look at us so she could tell them all about it when they woke up.

'Old,' said my mother as we walked towards the dining room. 'A lot old.'

'This is Mrs Shaw,' the girl told us.

Mrs Shaw was watching television while all around her slept. She had bright eyes and a built-in twinkle.

'Mrs Shaw watches the sport,' the girl added, 'all the time.'

'Do you like sport?' Mrs Shaw asked my mother.

'Rivelin,' said my mother. 'It has the contralone of the grapes with it all in muslin.'

'Come and sit here then, love, and watch it with me. It'll be nice to have someone to talk to.'

In the main lounge my mother's eyes took on a wary look as she examined yet another row of afternoon nappers. It was as though she had never thought of sharing the house with anyone else – there would be a lot of people here when they all woke up.

Margaret met us in the hallway and immediately gave my mother a big hug.

'I've heard so much about you,' she told her.

'That,' said my mother, pointing to the ceiling.

The young assistant explained.

'She rather fancies Mrs Mottram's room.'

Margaret's face had a few words with my mother. Her nose wrinkled in disbelief, her eyebrows linked elbows with one another and her lips just couldn't believe it.

One finger traced each step of the staircase through the air, at first dancing sprightly upwards and then collapsing, exhausted, before it reached the top.

'Come with me – let me show you.'

She took her arm and led her towards a door tucked away in the corner of the hallway. Once there she paused to heighten the tension and then pushed open the door with such a flourish that it really ought to have been accompanied by a fanfare.

It was a perfectly ordinary little room, well-lit by two large windows but with none of Mrs Mottram's style about it.

A single bed, a bedside table, a small wash-basin in the corner and a built-in wardrobe. The bed was stripped bare and the room looked as though we had taken it by surprise.

My mother sat down heavily on the edge of the bed and made no attempt to hide her disappointment.

'It's not,' she said sadly, and then went on to tell us what it wasn't.

Margaret listened carefully, crouching at her feet. She listened with her body, assuring my mother that she had an attentive audience and then, when the time was right, she stopped her in mid-stream by simply touching her hand. 'I'll remember that,' I thought.

Now it was time for the main performance. Margaret moved over to the far corner and drew a chair with her hands.

'Your chair – yours.'

She was by the window now where she pulled a small dressing table and a lovely little stool out of thin air. I could almost have sat on it.

Next she painted a new bedside table with a ripple of her fingers and placed upon it the most beautiful lamp anyone had ever imagined. My mother really liked that lamp and she was still admiring it when Margaret asked her to stand up.

'The bed goes,' she said, 'you bring your bed.'

My mother nodded and by the time Margaret flung open the wardrobe door we could almost see my mother's clothes hanging there, coats on the right, dresses on the left.

There was obviously more to come, but then my mother stepped in – it was her bloody room after all. She stopped Margaret in mid-flow by touching her hand – she learnt fast, and then she began to put her own personal touches to the place.

She moved the dressing table just a few inches to the left, it hadn't been central to the window, and pictures began to appear on the walls and her treasures covered the windowsills.

She waved her hand and a larger table appeared, sturdy enough to take her portable television. It was all coming along very nicely and a pink candlewick bedspread finished it off.

My mother sat down to admire her handiwork and then right on cue, as though he had been kept off-stage until this very moment, a small ginger cat strolled into the room to say hello.

'It's a Horace!' my mother cried.

That was a terrible slur on the little cat and he could have sued her for every penny she'd got, but he was a pleasant little soul and life was too short to harbour grudges.

So he just gave her a quick rub, said he'd see her later on and then went off to have a word with his other patients who were now waking up in bunches all over the place.

'Loved Whisky,' my mother told the young assistant whose bright smile turned into a worried frown at the thought of having an aged alcoholic about the place.

We rounded off the tour with a cup of tea in the kitchen and I managed a few brief moments alone with Margaret.

'Is the room available now?'

'Almost – by the weekend I should think.'

Nothing more needed to be said. In the wardrobe there had been real clothes hanging from real hangers. Not many – just a few dresses and the odd coat, all that would be needed by some old lady hanging on to the edge of life.

'Keep in touch,' she said. 'I'll let you know.'

*   *   *

Old ladies are a pretty tough breed and it was a fort-night before the call came. Aileen and I drove down to Chesterfield to see my mother through the move.

I was worried that she might have cold feet at the last minute. It wasn't going to be easy for her to turn her back on her own home for the very last time.

She was waiting for us. She sat on the settee with her best coat buttoned up to her neck and a little zip-top canvas shopping bag on her knee.

'Ready go,' she said and she was off towards the door.

'Hang on a minute.'

Aileen caught her hand and sat her down again.

'Have you got everything you want?'

She nodded and turned her bag upside down and her nightie fell out on to the floor followed by a spare pair of knickers and a bottle of Buttercup Syrup.

'That it?'

She shook her head and pushing her hand deep down into her coat pocket she produced a quarter of boiled sweets – Willet's Winter-mixture.

Whilst I ferried, first her bed and her chair up to Springbank, and then her more personal bits and pieces, Aileen took her, item by item, through her wardrobe. At last we had it all together and it was time to go.

She never looked back as she walked up the path and even though Aileen and I were choking with the emotion of the moment, my mother took it all in her stride – as though she was just nip-ping up to Henstocks for half a dozen iced cherry buns.

It was just the same as she walked in to her room. She wasn't at all surprised to see her own furniture in position – but then she had seen it all before in her imagination.

251

I had talked this moment over with Aileen until the early hours. We would stay with her for as long as it took to get her settled – she would need us to act as a buffer. When we felt the moment was right, then we would quietly disappear.

'Your tea's ready, Mrs Longden,' shouted a voice from the doorway and my mother was gone.

We waited a while and then I followed her and put my head around the dining-room door. She was seated at a round table with six other ladies and as they ate they listened intently to Mrs Shaw who told them all about the Belgian Grand Prix.

The little ginger cat sat by the side of my mother's chair and guarded her handbag, and in return for his services she fed him a continuous supply of boiled ham.

They made a good team and Margaret smiled as she watched them through the serving hatch. I was leaving her in good hands – the paws were a bonus.

Chapter 26

I hardly knew what to do with myself – for the first time in over seventeen years I was able to plan ahead and I wasn't used to it.

During the years with Diana I had spent my days and nights helping her to cope with one disaster after another, at the same time keeping a weather eye open for the next one on the list.

My life had been slotted into whatever time was left over and that had been time enough – but now there were vast acres of the stuff out there and I wasn't quite sure what to do with it all.

Aileen was full of ideas and most of them involved me climbing up ladders with a roller in one hand and a one-inch paintbrush in the other.

She also began to push me out into the world and those quick day-returns down to see the publishers in London were turned into a three-day thrash.

'We're going to a party.'

'What sort of party?'

'You'll see.'

I met some lovely people and I met some others. Faces that I had only seen before on book jackets and the television screen. I had long conversations with my heroes – well longish.

John Mortimer made a beeline towards me – from right across the room.

'Is that your glass?'

'No, it's not mine.'

'It's probably mine then.'

'Yes, it probably is.'

I suppose it was only a shortish conversation really, but I still remember it word for word.

Back at home my phone-calls went upmarket. Maureen Lipman rang to say she had loved the proof copy of my book and that husband Jack Rosenthal had read it in hospital.

'He wants a word with you.'

Here was my number one hero. I had *Bar Mitzvah Boy* on video and I'd watched it a dozen times. I held my breath.

'One of the best books I've read in ten years, love,' Jack told me and my ego did a quick-step on the ceiling and then broke into the Gay Gordons.

Maureen came back on the line.

'Mind you,' she said, 'he doesn't read many books.'

Bantam Press had suggested a change of title. I had called the book *Wide Eyed and Legless*, but Jim Cochrane came up with *Diana's Story* and I was happy enough with that. Then to my delight 'Woman's Hour' decided to serialize the book in eleven parts and producer Pat McLoughlin rang me to say she had found the perfect music.

'Andy Fairweather-Lowe's "Wide Eyed and Legless" – it's perfect.'

Pat abridged the book with such skill that it merely seemed to have gone on a diet and lost a few pounds – it was in good shape and she suggested I read it myself. At first I was reluctant.

'Perhaps an actor might make a better job of it.'

'Nonsense.'

She was very patient with me. She believed I could do the job and gradually her confidence rubbed off

254

on to me. She encouraged and coached me and I was frightened to death of her.

'You've done a lot of radio work, so don't worry – just let it go.'

I read the first episode beautifully, my voice bringing out the humour and the pathos, the light and the shade, and as I dropped the final sheet down on to the table I was almost overcome with the emotion of having discovered something within myself that almost amounted to genius.

Pat came in from the control room and sat opposite.

'That was amazing – you must be the first person to record a fifteen-minute episode in eight minutes seventeen seconds flat. Right, now let's start again . . . '

She was just what I needed – a perfectionist. A cross between my best friend and a Gestapo officer and she worked me to a standstill.

'That was very good – now let's try it again, only this time . . . '

I wasn't looking forward to recording the final episode. Diana had died too many times already without me going over it all again.

But Pat, whilst remaining as meticulous as ever, steered me through the session, adding an extra dollop of love and compassion for good measure and within a fortnight you could hardly see the bruises.

Aileen came down to London with me. She had a meeting the next day with her editor.

'Don't worry about me. You go and work with Pat – I'll stay here in the hotel and have a crack at the book.'

Her computer had to stay at home in Huddersfield and so I left her sitting on the bed, nibbling at the blunt end of a biro, shorthand notebook on her knee. She wouldn't be able to see what she had written, but I could read it back to her later on.

I went straight from the studio to another meeting and it was dark when I arrived back at the hotel.

'I've done fifteen pages.'

'That's good – let's go and eat first and then I'll read it back to you.'

We spoiled ourselves a little in celebration of a fair day's work and then I settled down to read aloud the opening pages of *Chapter of Echoes*. Aileen jumped up on the bed and pulled her knees tight under her chin, a model of concentration.

It wasn't as easy for me to concentrate – I could see the tops of her stockings – but I soldiered on and very soon I was into my stride.

I read the first two pages and then came to a stuttering halt at the top of page three. She looked up, wondering what was wrong, and I searched around to find a gentle way of telling her that her biro had run out halfway down the third page.

She took it very well.

'Oh dear,' she said – or words to that effect. Then she slipped off the bed, walked calmly over to the bathroom and locked herself in.

For a full five minutes there came sounds from that little room that I can only describe as the death throes of a lemming; and then she jumped back on the bed, picked up the pad, and started all over again.

I seemed to have cornered the market in spunky women.

Back at Springbank House it wasn't all sweetness and light. Most of the time my mother enjoyed being spoilt and looked after, but an idle life can be stretched only so far, then it stops bouncing back and just hangs there.

She was cut off from any real conversation. During the first few weeks she had smiled or nodded wisely whenever she was spoken to, but time found her sitting next to those old ladies who were really only talking into space and didn't require an answer anyway.

A perennial smile begins to hurt after a while and so eventually she restricted herself to the wise nod, winding even that down and putting it aside as she learnt that she didn't really have to listen at all.

The staff took time to talk with her and she sat for hours with them in the kitchen, but they were busy people and would have to dash away when an alarm bell rang. Sometimes they would have to leave her in the middle of one of her convoluted sentences and she would wonder why. What had she said? What had she done?

'I'm good, Jessie – I'm good.'

I tried hard not to feel guilty. I had done enough of that to last me a lifetime and this was the best I could do, apart from devoting my entire life to her. And she wouldn't want that – would she?

I had photocopied Aldous Huxley's foreword to *Brave New World* and stuck it on the lampshade over my desk.

'*Chronic remorse is a most undesirable sentiment . . . On no account brood over your wrongdoing. Rolling in the muck is not the best way of getting clean.*'

Good advice that, Aldous, and I'm doing my best. Is it all right if I just have a *little* roll every now and then?

She was having a nap when I called to see her. She was good at naps, she had practised for most of her life and now all that intensive training was beginning to pay off and she could nap with the best of them.

I woke her gently and she blinked a couple of times. Who the hell was this? And then recognition.

'Jessie!'

She rose unsteadily to her feet and I steered her across the lounge, through the hall and into her little bedroom so that she could launch herself into a monologue that would last a good three quarters of an hour.

This pattern remained constant. Every little moan had been stored up for when Jessie came and now it was poured out in a torrent.

'They cried it – they've got grains and it was well in – oh, they tained it. I vest – I vest, Jessie. They came up and they . . . '

She searched for the right word.

' . . . they grevved, polking all over – nisty buggers.'

To prove it she opened her handbag and showed me.

'Fan heaters gone.'

It certainly wasn't there now, the bag was empty. But she had outwitted them in the end – they couldn't fool her and she illustrated the lengths to which she had to go in order to foil their grevving and polking.

Falling first on to her hands and knees and then down on to her stomach, she inched herself under the bed and pulled back a corner of the carpet.

'Trim it, Jessie.'

I trimmed it and there, hidden away from all but the most nimble of geriatrics, were her comb, powder compact, lipstick, the smaller of two address books, an embroidered handkerchief and £1.27 in loose change.

For the first hour of my visit I would absorb her sadness in through my pores until, just as I reached saturation point, she would see me for the first time.

She would read her own sadness in my eyes, see it pouring out from the soles of my shoes and think – poor sod, what's happened to him?

Then she would try to cheer me up when all I wanted to do by this time was to curl up on the bed with my thumb stuck in my mouth and hide all my loose change under the carpet.

'What going, Jessie?'

'Baslow?'
'That's him.'

Nine times out of ten we went off to Baslow for a couple of hours. I found that if we repeated the same pattern time and time again then we were equals.

She knew the ice-cream van would be parked at the crossroads – her finger would be at the ready, waiting to flick the red button that released her seat belt.

She knew we would sit on the wall over there because then the scruffy old horse could creep up behind her and pinch her cornet – right out of her hand.

She knew I would shake my head – how could she let a horse steal her ice-cream? And she knew she would have a good laugh when the horse put his head over my shoulder and stole mine.

We didn't mind. There would be more ice-cream down in the village. We would sit at that table by the wall and watch the people in the cars as they pulled up at the traffic-lights. The young lovers in the battered mini.

'Aaah.'

The elegant woman in the Jaguar.

'Dainty.'

The smug yuppie in the Porsche with his Dire Straits cassette leaking out through his sun-roof.

'Flump.'

She knew that next on the list would be a tour of Chatsworth House and she knew every move the guide would make before he even thought of it. Those Americans over there didn't – but she did.

At Calver she would be out of the car and striding towards the Craft Shop before I could lock the passenger door. First a quick look at the pottery owls and then up a couple of steps and through a door. Come on, Jessie – the restaurant's through here, I know these things.

No need to study the menu – just point. That – had it last week and the week before – nice.

Very nice – better than last week. Delicious.

'Fine fart this, Jessie.'

She didn't hear the clatter of cake forks as they hit the floor or the embarrassed silence that followed. The collective grin was lost on her, as was the odd glance from Disgusted of Bakewell on table twelve over there.

This was her old stomping ground. There would be no surprises hiding round the corner, waiting to jump out at her and show her up as a fool.

On the way back to Springbank she could stride confidently into Loggins supermarket. She knew where they kept the Softmints and she could plonk the 20p I had given her down on the counter with confidence – no change you see. No need to talk, just a smile, just like the old days.

'Are you all right, love – feel better now?'

She beamed at me.

'Oh merrily.'

I loved that phrase. It was one she only brought out every now and then – she saved it for special occasions. It was all her own work and they were two of the loveliest words I had ever heard.

She was relaxed now and before I left we would have a nice chat, over a cup of tea, in the lounge at Springbank.

'You remember Sally?'

'Dobby?'

'Sally – your granddaughter.'

'Nick's son?'

'That's right. She's fallen in love with a blackjack-dealer from the casino.'

'Well they do, Jessie – I know these things.'

Taken twice a week my visits were quite therapeutic and I would leave her feeling much calmer and with all her tubes cleared out until the next time.

It wasn't that the staff failed her in any way, it was just that I was the only one who could understand every word she said.

She stood on the step and waved me goodbye.

'Take 'em, Jessie – they're growing for glow-worms under the grain.'

'OK, love – you know these things.'

Chapter 27

The phone never stopped ringing all day. First it was Sally from the Bahamas.

'You sound half asleep, Dad.'

'It's half past three in the morning.'

'Oh, I'm sorry I forgot – it isn't here.'

'Is anything wrong? Are you all right?'

'Yes, I'm fine. Dad – how would you like a kick-boxer for a son-in-law?'

'What happened to the blackjack-dealer?'

'It's the same one.'

'Did you say son-in-law?'

'Yes.'

At this point I took the phone into the kitchen and switched the kettle on.

'Is he safe?'

'He's lovely. His name's Steve and he's an ordinary boxer as well – you know, where they don't kick one another – and he plays karate.'

'You don't play karate – you play cricket.'

'He doesn't like cricket.'

My God – she must love him.

'Look, Sal – you talk and I'll listen.'

I listened for another thirty minutes. It must be costing her a fortune.

'Did you reverse the charges – I can't remember?'

'No.'

'Carry on then.'

'He wants me to come back to England with him. He has a share in a wine bar and we're going to run it together – it's in Oswestry.'

From the Bahamas, back to deepest Shropshire. 'Let me take you away from all this,' in reverse.
'Do you love him?'
'Yes – very much.'
'Then I'm very happy for you.'
'Thank you.'
'Sally?'
'Yes.'
'Wasn't there anybody normal in the Bahamas?'

I stayed up and worked until the milkman came and then I took Aileen a cup of tea in bed. I told her about Steve.
'He's probably a very nice kick-boxer,' she said and went back to sleep.

An hour later Nick rang from Dubai. He sounded chirpy and full of himself – happy as a sandboy.
'What's wrong, Nick?'
I knew him inside out.
'Nothing – I just didn't want you to worry.'
'What about?'
'It was nothing.'
'What wasn't?'
'The accident.'
'What accident?'
From that point on the conversation settled down somewhat and became less like a table tennis match.
'I fell off a motor bike in Thailand and broke my arm and my cigarette lighter got embedded in my thigh.'
Well, it happens to everyone sooner or later, doesn't it? I took the phone back in to the kitchen and put the kettle on once more.
'I'm all right now – I'm just limping a bit.'

Over the years I had come to terms with Nick and his accidents – disaster seemed to think that he was forever on heat.

As a toddler he spent his leisure hours sitting on a table in the Whitworth Hospital waiting for Sister Lane to come and stitch him up.

'What's he done this time?'

'Fallen off the washing-machine.'

'He did that last week.'

He did it every week. We never found out why he climbed up on to the washing-machine, how he climbed up on to the washing-machine or, having done so, why he hurled himself off the washing-machine. It was just something he did.

Diana worried about him night and day.

'I think you should fit him some stabilizers on that bike of his.'

'It's a three-wheeler – he can't fall off a three-wheeler.'

And he didn't. He rode it all the way down the stairs, through a plate-glass window and crashed into the rockery – but he didn't fall off.

As a child his hobby was collecting scabs all over his knees and then picking them off when they reached that interesting stage in their development.

'Don't do that, Nick.'

'All right.'

But he couldn't stop it – he was a scabaholic, he was hooked and his knees trembled with fear whenever he took his mittens off.

Then one day he stopped doing it, just like that, and Diana was so proud of him.

'I think he's growing up – becoming more responsible.'

'I don't trust him.'

And I was right. His mother lavished praise upon him and he took it all with a quiet smile and then one day I heard Sally talking to him in the bathroom.

'Mummy's very proud of you, Nicholas – you haven't picked your scabs for ages.'

'No – I'm saving them for my holidays.'

*   *   *

As a young man he had written off three cars in quick succession and on each occasion he was the innocent party. He was a good driver – it was just fate. Nick simply made himself available and other people drove straight at him.

'Are you sure you are all right?'

'Honest – I thought it best to wait until I'd recovered before I told you about it.'

'You'll do that on the day you get killed and it'll be too late. Next time ring me and let me worry.'

'OK.'

'What were you doing in Thailand?'

'I was on holiday – I had a wonderful time.'

'Even with a cigarette lighter embedded in your thigh?'

'Yes, it was great.'

'Are you really fit now?'

'Yes – I've given up smoking.'

Aileen and I tried to work but the phone had the bit between its teeth now and it wouldn't give up.

Jim Cochrane rang about the book cover.

'What's it look like?'

'Very good. The photograph of you and Diana isn't the best we could have wished for, but we've fuzzed it around the edges and I think it will pass.'

I couldn't wait to see myself fuzzed around the edges.

One by one Aileen's kids checked in. First it was Annie, the youngest, who could melt your heart just by looking at you – even down the phone.

Then it was David who liked nothing better than a deep intellectual conversation.

'Hello, David.'

'Hello.'

'How are you?'

'I'm fine, thank you – and you?'

'I'm fine, thank you.'

'That's good. Could I have a word with my mum?'

I enjoy a deep intellectual conversation as much as anyone – perhaps that's why we got on so well.

Paul didn't ring – he faxed us. He wasn't always like that. When I first met him he was a blond rock singer, a wild-haired heavy-metal man who wore obscene T-shirts.

Now he wore a sharp haircut and a business suit – he had crossed over. Then I read his fax aloud to Aileen and realized that perhaps he hadn't changed all that much, after all.

We only needed Helen to ring now and we would have the set. Helen was the oldest and sometimes the youngest – it just depended on how she felt.

I considered myself a very lucky man. I genuinely liked all four of them and they seemed to like me and the odds against that happening were enormous. They hadn't picked me and I hadn't picked them. Of course I was very lovable, but even so . . .

The phone rang again and for a few erotic moments I flirted outrageously with the young woman on the other end of the line.

'Who is that?' Aileen demanded.

'It's Helen – your daughter,' I told her and handed her the phone.

They were still at it an hour later and so I slipped up to bed. Sally had shortened what had passed for the night before by some four hours and I was shattered.

So when Aileen tiptoed into the bedroom a few minutes after midnight I was already in that wonderful half-world where sleep is looking after you personally – 'whenever you're ready, sir, just you take your time.'

I kept it waiting in the wings for a moment or so while Terry Wogan finished his big build-up.

'And now – let me introduce an author who has swept the board, winning both the Booker and the Whitbread prize in the same year – Deric Longden.'

As I walked out to a frenzied bout of artificial whooping and cheering Aileen walked across to the dressing table and began taking off her clothes.

'Yer must have been absolutely thrilled,' Terry began, *'to have won so many honours in such a short time and now a little bird tells me that a film . . .'*

There is a remoteness about the way Aileen takes her clothes off – as though she were performing on a stage herself. It has to do with her being blind. She doesn't examine a single garment as she unbuttons and removes it, there's little point – she can't see it and so she ignores it.

She looks straight ahead, into the middle distance as though into the eyes of an invisible audience.

' . . . about to be made, based on your book . . .'

For God's sake, shut up, Terry – we're just getting to the best bit.

'I'm sorry – pardon me for breathing.'

She is one of the few women I have known who look as good with their clothes off as they do with them on and she was coming over to see if I was really asleep.

I lay with my head on the pillow, my eyes half open. Lit by the lamp, low on the bedside table, she tiptoed across the carpet until she was standing over me – then she bent until our noses were a whisker's breadth apart. Even at that distance she couldn't make out whether my lids were closed or not and so she backtracked to the dressing table to wipe off her make-up.

It's an unnerving experience being examined at such close quarters like that and perhaps I should have let her in on the secret, but I was enjoying this drowsy half-world and the show wasn't over yet.

As she opened the mirrored door of the wardrobe her reflection was cast over several screens – the three faces of the winged mirror on the dressing table and the glass top of the Chinese table.

She pulled open a second wardrobe door and now there were seven naked Aileens dancing in the bedroom. It was Fantasy Island.

'Are yer ready yet?' Terry wanted to know.

If you don't mind I'll give it a miss this time – ask me again when the paperback comes out.

'I don't suppose there's much point in me hanging around,' whispered Sleep with an understanding smile.

Not really. I'm sorry – I've kept you waiting.

'That's all right – I'll call back later.'

It was to be much, much later.

In the best of movie traditions Aileen lay in my arms as together we shared both a cigarette and that wonderful weightless moment that destroys all the arguments of the celibate – that moment afterwards, when two people feel as close as one and all the loose ends of love are drawn up tight.

I loved her very much and she knew it and felt safe. That's what I wanted for her – to feel secure and not have to look over her shoulder any more.

'What did Helen have to say?'

'Oh, I didn't tell you, did I?'

'No.'

'You'll never believe it.'

'I will – it's Helen we're talking about.'

'She's got engaged.'

'That's two in one day.'

'His name is John McDonald – he's the World Light-Heavyweight Tae Kwondo-Do Champion.'

The girls were bringing in the heavy artillery. Still, he might come in very handy if this Steve turned awkward.

*   *   *

We settled down with heavy eyes and the pillows came up to meet us. Some nights I just don't know what to do with my arms. It's as though they've never done this before and I'm no help because I can't remember where I usually put them.

Not tonight though. They slipped into place like a couple of pros and my legs took note and followed suit. Slowly my body sank into the mattress and the duvet sighed and snuggled up against my cheek.

Then the phone rang and I could have cried.

'Hello?'

It was Margaret from Springbank House.

'I am sorry to have to ring you at this time, Deric.'

'What's wrong?'

'Your mum's had an accident, I'm afraid. She fell down the stairs and we think she's broken her hip – they've taken her to the Derbyshire Royal at Calow.'

'How is she?'

'She's very poorly.'

I put the phone down and then I did cry.

Chapter 28

I pulled off the dual carriageway, swung round left in a wide arc, turned right at the traffic lights and then pumped up the steep hill towards the hospital.

As I cut through a brief strip of countryside my headlights picked out a young hedgehog snuffling across the road. He stopped for a moment to consider the situation, thanked me with a curt nod and then carried on as I eased the car to a halt. A phone rang in my head.

'Deric?'

'Yes, love.'

'There's a little hedgehog sitting on my lawn – he's been there all afternoon. Do you think he's all right?'

'I don't know – I thought they were nocturnal.'

'No, this one isn't – it's more sort of oval.'

I sat by her bed and held her hand. There would be no more oval hedgehogs. She lay still, half doped, groaning every now and then as she stared at a point above my left shoulder.

'Jessie,' she muttered.

'I'm here, love.'

'Jessie,' she shook her head very slowly and shivered.

A nurse appeared behind me and my mother pulled a sheet up over her head and hid behind it.

She hadn't been able to tell them where it hurt or ask them what they were doing, and they hadn't been able to tell her what they were doing, when they were doing it or why. They had hurt her even more. They shouldn't do that, should they? Not nurses.

*   *   *

Some days later they took her down a long corridor and she thought she was going home.

'Spongo?'

'Yes, that's right, Mrs Longden – Spongo.'

At the end of the corridor they put her to sleep and gave her a plastic hip and now they wanted her to walk.

'You've got to get used to it, Mrs Longden.'

But it hurt. They couldn't know how much it hurt – they wouldn't ask her to try if they knew. Must make them understand.

'It's no good ranting on like that, Mrs Longden – it's got to be done.'

Jessie would tell them – he would tell them to leave her alone. But even Jessie didn't seem to understand. He sided with the nurses – Jessie was a big disappointment.

So she stopped talking. What was the point? She lay on her side and stared at the wall until I arrived, and then she would stare at me with eyes so dull they seemed to have been turned down with a dimmer-switch.

I watched as two nurses changed her bedding – one either side of the bed.

They were talking over her, through her and round her. They talked of boy-friends and girl-friends, never seeming to notice the old woman who had somehow become mixed up with the sheets. She had lost all identity – she was just that crabby old woman who lay on her side and faced the wall.

I tried to paint a picture of the real woman behind those dead eyes. A woman who rarely criticized and never envied, just simply loved almost everyone and everything. A woman who could perceive goodness even when it was well hidden and who saw beauty in a cat with just one nostril and a single ear.

271

But the nurses only half listened – they were too young. What were they? Twenty? Twenty-two? Would I have looked far beyond those eyes at that age? No, of course I wouldn't.

The next day I called at the old house. It stood as my mother had left it with everything in place – her chair pulled up to the television, a spare bottle of Buttercup Syrup in the kitchen cupboard. The house was there as a fail safe if Springbank House hadn't worked out, or maybe she might like to spend the odd day in her old surroundings.

But once she had walked out of the front door she never mentioned it again, not even as we had sailed past the end of the road on our day trips to Baslow and Chatsworth House.

There was a cat sitting on the doorstep.

'I've heard good reports about this place.'

'Sorry, old son – it's closed for the duration.'

On the top shelf of a wardrobe I found a box of old photographs, and tipping them out on to the floor I embarked on a journey back through time. There was my mother, heavily pregnant – me as a lump. It was slightly blurred, maybe I had moved.

I found the photograph I wanted and took it downstairs. There on the mantelpiece, in a gilded frame, the lump was now wearing a white angora bonnet and little white bootees. I pulled the back from the frame and replaced him with the picture from the box. It was a shame in a way – it was a very cute little lump.

Her eyes hadn't even flickered at the sight of the Buttercup Syrup. I had hoped for more than that – perhaps I could borrow a spoon and we could get stoned together – but no, the eyes started out in the general direction of the bottle but never quite made the journey, tailing off halfway as though the battery was running down.

A nurse pushed a tall pill-trolley to the end of the bed and began filling a little plastic tub. She double-checked the dosage and then sat on the edge of the bed.

'Here we are, Mrs Longden – shall we sit up?'

Mrs Longden had to be hauled up by the two of us, one each side, and she groaned with the pain, but she took the pills meekly enough and then stayed put, gazing blankly at her hands.

'Who's this?' the nurse asked me, reaching over to the locker and taking down a photograph in a gilded frame. 'She's beautiful – is it her daughter?'

'No – it's my mother,' I told her, nodding at the bed. 'It's her.'

'Really?'

She studied the woman in the photograph. The woman was quite something, tall and slender, about eighteen years old. She wore a slim-fitting coat with a fur collar and black hair spilled on her shoulders. The ankles gave more than a clue to the quality of the hidden legs above and the face was quite simply stunning, elegant and sophisticated, yet at the same time fresh and eager.

'Who's that?'

Another nurse had joined us and was reaching out for the photograph.

'It's Mrs Longden.'

'Is it really? She looks lovely – I fancy that coat, I could wear that now.'

My mother's eyes were taking in the scene. She recognized the frame – it was Jessie when he was a baby. The nurse turned the photograph so that my mother could see it.

'You were beautiful, Mrs Longden.'

A tiny spark of life flickered in her eyes, not enough to ease away the sorrow lines in that sad face but enough to bring a smile to mine.

'Tame,' she said wearily, pointing at the photograph.

'That's right,' the nurse agreed, 'it's you.'

When the shifts changed over the new nurses picked up the photograph and saw for themselves just a glimpse of the real woman behind the twisted tongue and the addled brain and they talked to her as they changed her dressing.

I broke open the Buttercup Syrup and my mother licked her lips as she sipped it from a plastic teaspoon. It was time for a small celebration and she gave a weak smile as I raised the bottle in salute.

At the very least we had clawed back a little piece of her identity. She was no longer something that had come along with the bedding – she was the woman in the photograph.

I had been to Oswestry once before to report on a football match. I had memories of driving rain, a hot-dog stall behind one goal and a telephone that actually worked.

Aileen remembered an army camp, Nissen huts and a honeymoon that almost worked.

Now we were looking for the Good Companion wine bar and on our third circuit of the town we found it tucked away around a bend in Beatrice Street. It was a pretty place. Once, a long, long time ago, it had been an ironmonger's shop and the old counter was now a bar.

Behind it stood a young woman with blue-black hair. She was about to embark on a journey to the table by the window and she balanced three lasagnes, a stuffed pepper and a carafe of red wine as though she had been doing this all her life.

'Hi, Sal.'

She started, looked up in surprise and then juggled with the three lasagnes, the stuffed pepper and the red wine as though she hadn't been juggling very long at all.

'Sir – madam. If you would like to sit down at that table over there, I will come and play hell with you in a few moments.'

We sat down and looked around. Tight by the side of us a young man stood at the next table, notepad in his hand, as he went through the menu for the benefit of three young women who stared up at him adoringly.

'That's him – I'm sure it is,' I whispered, 'that's the kick-boxer.'

Aileen leant over until she was almost horizontal, her nose an inch away from the seat of his pants. For a moment I thought she was going to fall over and then she swung back again like the needle of a metronome.

'Nice bum,' she said.

She should know, she could have bitten it. At least she hadn't taken out her magnifying glass.

He had the young women in the palm of his hand now and he was enjoying every minute of it. He went through the menu once again just to make sure – he certainly gave value for money – and then Sally swung past carrying a tray of dirty dishes and as she inched by him she gave the bum a firm pinch.

My bum once had a personality all of its own and attracted a certain amount of attention – now I just sat on it.

I watched Sally as a customer paid his bill. She had that old sparkle back again – more than that, she had grown into a new woman with an aura of self-confidence around her. If Steve was responsible then I could forgive him anything – even his bum.

He was at the other end of the bar pouring drinks. He was tall and he was handsome and although there was a distance between them it was only in feet and inches. You could tell they belonged together. They were a couple and you would have to be blind not to notice it.

'They seem just right for one another,' I told Aileen.

'I know,' she said, 'I can feel it.'

The food was good and we ate the lot. We had to. Every few minutes an anxious face would peer around the door of the kitchen to see how we were getting on.

'For God's sake, don't leave anything,' I told Aileen.

'Why not?'

'It must be Guy, Steve's brother – he's almost a carbon copy and he keeps having a look to see if we're enjoying it.'

'I'll eat it all.'

'And if you could smile while you swallow, it would be a great help.'

They kept Guy chained up in the kitchen where he was the master of all he surveyed. It hurt him if customers left any of his food and he was better tucked well away from them.

But they let him out at closing time and the three of them joined us with a couple of bottles from behind the bar and an enormous black Dobermann called Senator.

Sally was frightened of dogs, she always had been and this one was more like a pit pony. It made a pass at my bread roll and then tried to sit on my knee.

'Sit,' ordered Sally.

'It is doing,' I told her, as best I could with a jet-black ear sticking up my nose, and she sighed and fearlessly hauled it off into a back room where it played with two white kittens called Gizmo and Stripe. It's amazing what love can do.

*   *   *

We talked long into the night. Steve and Guy were good company and across the table Sally and Aileen sat in a close huddle. I watched them with increasing pleasure. There was none of that plastic politeness about them now, they had their heads together and there was a conspiracy in the air.

'We're getting married in July,' Sally announced, 'I shall be Sally French – I like that.'

'Congratulations – am I invited?'

'If you're good – what about you two?'

'What about us?'

'Isn't it about time you stopped living in sin? It's not nice for a daughter.'

I looked across at Aileen. We had thought about it and had talked about it and we wanted it. We felt like a couple as well – but how long was a decent interval?

'Next year,' Aileen said, 'sometime next year.'

Sally gave her a big hug and Steve disappeared to fetch another bottle. Sally watched him fondly as he walked towards the bar.

'What do you think, Dad?'

'I like him – I couldn't have wished for better.'

'Neither could I – smooth bugger, isn't he?'

Aileen nodded in agreement.

'Reminds me of your father,' she said.

We were woken the next morning by the sound of a Dobermann eating a wine glass on the landing.

'Your dog ate the rest,' I told Sally as I handed her the stem.

'Save washing-up, I suppose,' she sighed and dropped it in the bin. 'I'm so pleased about you and Aileen.'

'Are you really – it isn't just an act?'

'Does it look like an act?'

'No.'

'And it isn't. She's lovely – anyone can see that you were made for one another – Mum would be pleased.'

'Do you think so?'

'I know so – she said something about it to Rosie Cuff.'

I wanted to know more, but then Guy hurtled downstairs. He was attached at the wrist to a large Dobermann and together they shot out of the door and headed off along Beatrice Street.

Steve, wrapped up in a white robe, padded down at a more sedate pace. Both his eyes were still half-closed as an economy measure.

'I – er. The, table is – er, kettle,' he declared and made for the kitchen to pour coffee on his tongue.

Aileen followed him at a steady pace.

'It's drink,' she croaked as she disappeared round the kitchen door, 'Steve, it's the – er, and me Steve.'

'How *is* Nana?' Sally asked and I wondered what on earth could have prompted her. 'I want to see her, but I can't get away for a week or so.'

'She's fine,' I told her. No point in worrying her any more than I had to. 'She had a nasty fall, but she's a lot better now.'

'Really – are you sure?'

'Honest,' I said. 'She's fine.'

She died the next morning. I arrived just too late and the sister met me at the ward door.

'She just slipped away in her sleep,' she told me. 'She knew nothing about it and really it was what she wanted – I think it was for the best.'

'Perhaps it's for the best.'

Only my mother could have got away with a line like that when I had told her of Diana's death and now the sister was using the same phrase about her.

But this time it had the ring of truth about it.

'It's a long, long, lonely world.'

Her world had really come to an end the day her brain had stopped receiving and her tongue

278

had stopped transmitting – all the rest had been an unwanted extension.

'Could I see her?'

'Of course.'

She looked so peaceful. All the strain had gone out of her face, the frown had disappeared and her mouth had creased back into that slight smile I had missed so much.

The years had fallen away and she was that woman in the photograph once more – older and wiser, but still the same woman. Both there on the locker and here on the bed.

'Much bickier now.'

I cried as I held her hand but, as the tears ran down my cheek, I knew she wouldn't want that. She believed in another world and she had never been frightened of going there.

I was crying for myself. Christ take care of her – Christ, I would miss her! I gave her a final kiss and her skin was smooth to my lips.

'Are you happy now, Mum?'

'Oh, merrily,' she seemed to say. *'Oh, merrily.'*

I locked the door of her house and left it as it stood – I could sort that out sometime or other, but not yet. I simply took a few of her favourite bits and pieces so that I could have them around me, the elegant regency buck with the matchstick in his neck, the anxious sheep and the three-legged dog.

I popped the shepherd boy in the box, he would see that they came to no harm and then I took a second look at him and went back for his head.

At home I carried the box of old photographs upstairs and placed them on a shelf in the underdrawings. I could do without the pain of going through them right now, the time would come – but not yet.

The box nuzzled up to another box, a white box with a white butterfly engraved on the lid. It seemed so long ago that I had carried this upstairs and hidden it away.

'I'll go through them later – but not yet.'

Perhaps it was time I did. I laid the box on the bed and flipped off the lid. There was Diana, in a bikini in Ibiza. There she was again, in a wheelchair at Nick's wedding. Now she had a baby in her arms – it was Sally, and there was a three-year-old Sally, in wellingtons, swinging a red bucket around her head. There was Nick, aged four, driving a baby BMW in Belgium and there he was again, aged twenty-four, posing against a clapped-out Cortina in Matlock.

There was Diana dancing in a black dress – and there, slipped in amongst the photographs, was a diary. A black diary that had gone everywhere with her. I had never opened it – it was hers.

I took it downstairs and it sat on my desk for an hour before I began to turn the pages.

A whole month had been dismissed with bold strokes slashed right across the pages and qualified by the single word *Hospital*. Many weeks had been written off with the explanation *Pain*. There were days which were just *Lousy* and days that were *Lovely*, but there were other days.

'Wonderful day at Buxton with Deric. Bought ring from Liz Tye – collapsed on way home. Enjoyed it though.'

'Party at Brian and Gill's. Very happy. Danced with Brian – fell over. Broke my wrist?'

Excursions were the exception, however, most of her life was lived on the phone.

'Rang Aileen (sexy voice). Told her Deric depressed, needs convincing he has talent. Right she said.'

'Spent hour on phone with Aileen. Have worked out plan.'

'Deric gone to Chichester Conference with Aileen. Borrowed my bikini – Aileen not Deric.'

'Spent day with Aileen. She's easy to love – think she loves him as much as I do.'

'Deric on "Woman's Hour". Rang Aileen and we lis-
tened together.'

I put down the diary and sat quietly for a while. If I was honest with myself I was looking for approval – Diana's approval to set the seal on my new life.

I picked up the phone and rang Rosie Cuff. What was it Sally had said?

'Mum would be pleased . . . she said something about it to Rosie Cuff.'

'Hello, Rosie – it's Deric.'

'Hi, stranger.'

I mustn't go fishing. Perhaps Rosie had forgotten all about it – better not to know than to try and force her memory and finish up with some dim and hazy recollection that had been dug out purely to make me feel better.

We talked for a while of times past, gradually moving up to the late eighties and then Rosie asked: 'How's Aileen?'

'She's fine,' I said. 'We're thinking of getting married next year.'

There – that was the best I could do. It was up to Rosie now.

'That's wonderful,' she said, 'Diana would have been so pleased.'

'She would?'

'Oh yes. She once said to me, when she was very ill, she said – if anything happens to me I hope Deric marries Aileen. She'd be so right for him.'

Rosie moved on to other things but I can't for the life of me remember what they were and eventually, after we had squeezed the conversation dry, she brought it to a halt.

'Bye, Deric.'

'Bye, Rosie.'

And thank you, Rosie – and thank you, Diana.

*   *   *

I had a bookcase in my office that I had selected with great care the day after Jim Cochrane had accepted my first five chapters. It was a replica of the one that nestled up against the wall in Aileen's study.

On the top shelf she had twenty-five hardbacks, all written by herself. On the middle shelf were the same twenty-five in paperback and down at the bottom, dozens of foreign translations – *Hawksmoor* in Italian, *A Scent of Violets* in Norwegian and *Hawksmoor* again in a strange language called American.

Mine stood empty and waiting. It was to remain a virgin until I could place the first copy of *Diana's Story* on the top shelf and I had two book-ends ready and champing at the bit.

Most mornings I gave it a quick rub down with a mist of Pledge and a soft duster and it stood there as a silent reminder of my goal; glowering at me when things were not going well and giving me an imperceptible nod of encouragement when they were. Some days I felt like throwing it out of the window.

Waiting for a book to be published is like having a baby. It would be nine months before we heard the patter of tiny pages trotting through the letter-box, and the bookcase shuffled its shelves in boredom and I was a martyr to morning sickness.

Then one lunchtime there was a dull thud as a Transworld jiffy bag hit the hall carpet. At first, disappointment – it was too thin to be a book – and then the joyous thrill of holding my very first book jacket in my hand.

I laid it down on the hearthrug and stroked it gently, its coat was smooth and glossy. I read it twice from cover to cover, if you can read a cover from cover to cover, and then I slipped the jacket from Ned Sherrin's anthology *Cutting Edge*, and replaced it with mine.

It fitted beautifully and I laid the book on my desk and lit it from overhead with an angle-poise lamp. The gold of the title glared under the white light but after a small adjustment it settled down and I stood and stared in wonder. They had been right to fuzz the photograph and I tried not to look at that.

'What are you doing?' Aileen stood behind me.

'My book jacket's come.'

'Let me feel.'

She took it from me and ran her fingers over the slightly raised title.

'What's that on the back?'

'It's me.'

I was seated at a BBC radio console so ancient it was probably a wood-burning model.

'You look very handsome.' Thank God she was blind. 'Put it on your bookcase.'

'It's not my book – it's just the cover.'

'It doesn't matter.'

'That would be cheating.'

'So cheat.'

I placed it on the top shelf with the book-ends either side and then stood back.

'Looks all right, doesn't it?'

'It's beautiful. Diana would be proud of you.'

'She would, wouldn't she.'

'Very.'

I had written it as a celebration of Diana's life. She had no headstone – this I hoped would be her memorial.

Aileen slipped her hand in mine. She knew that to me, this was much more than just a book.

'It looks a bit lonely,' she said.

'It does, doesn't it.'

'Why don't you write another one – about your mother?'

'I might do that.'

*   *   *

The next morning I switched on my trusty Amstrad and after a while I began to write.

'I would have recognized that backside anywhere. It loomed large above the surprisingly slim ankles . . .'

Publisher's Note

Deric Longden's book Diana's Story *was published in June* 1989 *and before long appeared on* The Sunday Times *bestseller list. At the time of publication Deric Longden read an abridged version of the book on BBC Radio's 'Woman's Hour'. In March 1990 it was announced that the judges of the prestigious NCR Award had awarded* Diana's Story *a special prize.*

DIANA'S STORY
by Deric Longden

'A remarkable book, warm and sad . . . laced with a lot
of humour'
Sunday Express

In 1971 Deric Longden's wife Diana fell ill with the
mysterious disorder known as ME (myalgic encepha-
lomyelitis). She was unable to move without a
wheelchair, and was in almost constant pain. Equally
distressing, perhaps, was the fact that every doctor she
saw was unable to diagnose what was wrong with her.
Deric, devoting more and more time to looking after
Diana, watched his business gradually fail, and had to
neglect his developing career as a broadcaster. He
became house husband, nurse and caretaker of the
woman he loved.

Diana's Story, far from being one of gloom and despair,
ia poignant, courageous, and frequently moving. Told
by a writer who can transform the bleakest moments
with his warmth and wit, it is an extraordinary funny
account of a marriage based on love and on an
exceptional sense of humour.

'A funny, sad and, above all, enormously inspiring
story'
Clare Francis

Now the BBC Television drama *Wide-Eyed & Legless*,
starring Julie Walters, Jim Broadbent and Thora Hird.

0 552 13944 0

THE CAT WHO CAME IN FROM THE COLD
by Deric Longden

Deric Longden had never thought of himself as a cat lover, but from the moment he saw the tiny kitten sitting on an upturned bucket down in the garden he was hooked. Strictly speaking, the little cat belonged to the neighbours, but somehow when it began to rain it seemed only natural to bring him inside, and once there he slipped so easily into Deric's and Aileen's lives that there was an unspoken agreement that he had found his real home. Little did he know that he had entered the Longden world, in which ordinary life is always just a little out-of-the-ordinary.

Aileen being Aileen, it was probably inevitable that sooner or later the kitten would be trapped in the refrigerator for longer than was good for him. And Deric being Deric, the obvious way to thaw him back to life was to make a little coat for him out of an old thermal vest. Thus the cat who came in from the cold got his name – 'Thermal' – and joined the wonderful cast of characters in the ongoing Longden saga.

The Cat Who Came in from the Cold combines Deric Longden's unique style of gentle humour with all the comic solemnity and cuddly charm of an irresistible kitten.

0 552 13822 3

A SELECTION OF AUTOBIOGRAPHIES AND BIOGRAPHIES AVAILABLE FROM CORGI BOOKS AND BLACK SWAN

❒	14248 2	LIVE FROM THE BATTLEFIELD	*Peter Arnett*	£6.99
❒	99065 5	THE PAST IS MYSELF	*Christabel Bielenberg*	£6.99
❒	99469 3	THE ROAD AHEAD	*Christabel Bielenberg*	£6.99
❒	13741 3	LETTER TO LOUISE	*Pauline Collins*	£6.99
❒	14093 7	OUR KATE	*Catherine Cookson*	£5.99
❒	13582 8	THE GOD SQUAD	*Paddy Doyle*	£6.99
❒	13928 9	DAUGHTER OF PERSIA	*Sattareh Farman Farmaian*	£5.99
❒	99479 0	PERFUME FROM PROVENCE	*Lady Fortescue*	£6.99
❒	12833 3	THE HOUSE BY THE DVINA	*Eugenie Fraser*	£6.99
❒	14185 2	FINDING PEGGY: A GLASGOW CHILDHOOD	*Meg Henderson*	£6.99
❒	99637 8	MISS McKIRDY'S DAUGHTERS WILL NOW DANCE THE HIGHLAND FLING	*Barbara Kinghorn*	£6.99
❒	13944 0	DIANA'S STORY	*Deric Longden*	£4.99
❒	13822 3	THE CAT WHO CAME IN FROM THE COLD	*Deric Longden*	£4.99
❒	14301 4	ENOUGH TO MAKE A CAT LAUGH	*Deric Longden*	£5.99
❒	14050 3	I'M A STRANGER HERE MYSELF	*Deric Longden*	£4.99
❒	14544 0	FAMILY LIFE	*Elisabeth Luard*	£6.99
❒	13356 6	NOT WITHOUT MY DAUGHTER	*Betty Mahmoody*	£5.99
❒	13953 X	SOME OTHER RAINBOW	*John McCarthy & Jill Morrell*	£6.99
❒	14127 5	BRAVO TWO ZERO	*Andy McNab*	£5.99
❒	14288 3	BRIDGE ACROSS MY SORROWS	*Christine Noble*	£5.99